ADVANCE PRAISE

"Reframes AI as a mirror rather than a master, and hands creators back their agency in the process. Essential reading for anyone building a creative life alongside the machines."

— JOANNA PENN, *THE CREATIVE PENN*

"If you're an artist – or anyone who works in a creative field – who's curious about how AI can be harnessed for good, check out this book."

— *REEDSY DISCOVERY*

"One of the most thoughtful and intellectually honest books I've read on artificial intelligence."

— *GOODREADS REVIEWER* ★★★★★

WHAT MACHINES CAN'T REPLACE

WHY AI MAKES US MORE HUMAN

ANNA MCPHEE

Foreword by
ANDY POLAINE

E.
E.
PRESS

First published in 2026 by E. E. Press, Victoria, Australia

ISBN 978-1-7645848-1-4 (paperback)

ISBN 978-1-7645848-2-1 (hardback)

ISBN 978-1-7645848-0-7 (ebook)

Cover design by Pipeline Design

A note on AI: This book was written by Anna McPhee. Generative AI was used during its production as a research assistant and discussion partner, and to index and cross-reference the author's own notes and voice recordings. Any research it surfaced was checked by the author against the original sources, which are listed in the Notes and Bibliography. AI was not used to generate the text. Every sentence in this book was written and revised by the author. The cover was designed by human hand at Pipeline Design.

All inquiries should be made to the author at hello@anna.kiwi

For Emily, always. My greatest inspiration in everything I do.

"We shape our tools, and thereafter they shape us."

— JOHN M. CULKIN

CONTENTS

FOREWORD

ANDY POLAINE

If you're the kind of person who is impatient or always short on time, but still reads the foreword of books before considering a purchase, let me save you some time. Buy this book. It's an absolute joy.

If you feel like slowing down, here's the reason why.

For more decades than I'm willing to admit, I have always been fascinated by the way technology and culture interact with each other. Specifically, why some technologies are immediately absorbed, while others fall by the wayside. Why did email become such a staple of our modern world, yet be considered for "old people" by the following generation? Why did e-scooters proliferate on our streets and, somewhat irritatingly, pavements, when the Segway remained a novelty? The list of these is as long as human culture.

I remember encountering the pseudo-therapist program, ELIZA, when I was about 10 years old on my school's BBC Micro computer. I was fascinated by how easy it was to fall into the trap of anthropomorphising it, as much as it was fun to probe its structure, send it into loops and reveal itself as nothing more than a battery of stock phrases triggered by keywords. My 10-year-old self was both disappointed at how simple the magic trick was and fascinated by the fact that I had, for a few minutes, fallen for it.

45 years later, I recognise I have had a similarly ambivalent relationship with technology ever since. I feel drawn to explore it, but loathe simply believing in it wholesale without critical thought. I don't think I have ever encountered a technology that evinces such strong attraction and repulsion as AI. In the space of three or four years, its brand has transformed from wunderkind to devil's spawn in the public discourse.

I have railed against the "slopsided marketplace" in which plenty of people espouse their productivity efficiencies by using AI to triage email and Slack messages, but know of no one who enjoys being on the receiving end of AI-generated messages, LinkedIn posts and comments.

I have taken frequent aim at the greed for speed. Velocity, whether in coding, feature releases or business, in general, has become an unquestioned Good Thing. But apart from startups that genuinely do run out of money if they don't get to market, most organisations have no real need for the pressure of speed they inflict on everyone tasked with achieving it. Releasing products and services that are shoddy or, worse, cause harm, brings few advantages, only distrust and loathing from customers and users. Using AI to simply do more of the same, faster, is a lost opportunity to explore what only it can do and damaging when it atrophies our critical thinking faculties.

And yet, like many others with similar sentiments, I still find myself regularly using AI, just not relying on it. Claude has been a helpful health and fitness coach. I used it to re-build a website for my deceased father's artwork, because I wanted to experiment with Claude Code and the website had been on my to-do list for three years. And it is extremely useful for digging through German laws and regulations which are opaque even to native speakers.

I have so far kept it away from my writing, fearing the pollution of LLM tics, such as "not to, but to..." or "the honest question worth asking is...". I do, however, use it as a dialogue partner while developing the story arcs and scenes for my Dungeons & Dragons game that I have been dungeon mastering for the past five years. In a game that happens once a week in three-hour sessions, set in an imaginary world with its own lore, history and pantheon, it's easy to forget events and relationships that happened over the months. AI makes for an excellent lore-keeper.

Once or twice I've used Claude to generate a scene for my players, either up front during my prep or on the fly when they decided to do something I had not planned for. Each time I felt like a cheat. Empty. Like gorging myself on fast food only to be hungry 30 minutes later because it lacked any real nutrition. This sensation felt both mental and physical. I could feel something akin to shame, though disappointment in myself is perhaps a closer description. That plus a kind of physical and mental emptiness. I remain curious as to why that should be.

Since then, I still keep AI away from my professional writing, but I've switched my D&D usage of it to be that of a sparring partner. Claude's suggestions are mostly accurate in terms of the lore, but bland in terms of developing the game's excitement and tension. It simply has no sense of what a scene or character would *feel* like. But its misses help me recognise where my own thinking is at and spark original ideas in me. It's as if the AI paints the negative space so that I can see the ideas in my head that were there all along.

In *What Machines Can't Replace: Why AI Makes Us More Human* Anna McPhee examines why and how this process works. She manages an apparently effortless combination of poetic reflection on what it means to be a human, creating things in the world, and rigorous scientific examination of our relationship to technology, cognition and AI. She explores the boundary between fast and slow, between assistance and replacement. Anna calls this "the fence" between AI in her life and work. Certain activities, such as things that bring joy to do by hand or are critical to maintaining a critical mind and a healthy soul, are off-limits, while dull drudgery or preparation work are farmed out to AI. It leaves her to do what a human does well and the machine to do what the machine does well.

This relationship is as carefully cultivated as her garden that she often references in the book. I love gardens as metaphors for developing products and services because they are never finished. Nobody says, "We've shipped the garden." They are ecosystems in which each part affects the whole and they require *tending*. A shrub planted with good intentions thrives so much that it accidentally becomes a large tree, blocking the precious sunlight the tomatoes in Northern Europe so desperately need. Do we cut down the tree or plant the tomatoes somewhere else? And why hasn't the rosemary grown at all while the mint is now out of control like a weed? A big tech growth-at-speed mindset would simply plant bamboo everywhere and if you've ever had that in your garden, you'll know what a disastrous idea that is.

The tending to the AI relationship fence and what Anna describes as the contract between her and it also reminded me of my years of teaching. Drawing upon the Socratic Method, Clean Language and Motivational Interviewing, Anna describes her contract with AI: "You accelerate tasks; I protect slowness. You show me possibilities; I choose. You ask; I answer."

It is often painful to watch a student flounder in the execution of a piece of design work or my daughter with dyscalculia struggle to wrap her brain around the abstractions of maths. Operating from a position of greater knowledge and experience, it can be so tempting to just jump in and do it for them. To get the struggle over and done with. But doing so robs the student or my daughter of their agency, of the moment of triumph when they overcome the friction and finally manage it themselves. It takes patience and discipline as a teacher to avoid this. I frequently fail at both, as my daughter would be quick to tell you.

AI is designed to do tasks for you, to deliver finished results as sycophantically and quickly as possible. But, as Anna describes, in giving up this friction we leave ourselves empty. Ironically we need to teach the AI teacher to hold back from giving us the solution. In the final section of this book, Anna provides a set of activities for various creators, from visual artists to writers, filmmakers, musicians, developers and teachers. They are not prescriptive, but, rather, thought-provoking prompts to develop your own contract with AI. I'm looking forward to trying them out.

I've written a few forewords to books. The ask usually comes necessarily late in the process (I'm writing this just a few weeks before it will be published), since the final manuscript needs to be in place. This often means a speed read and it would, of course, be tempting to ask AI to do this for me. I did not for two reasons.

The first is the aforementioned fence that still separates my professional writing from AI. The second, more compelling reason, is that I enjoyed this book so much I wanted to slow down and savour it properly. I urge you to do the same and wish you the same feeling I had, akin to biting into the deliciously chewy crust of homemade sourdough topped with honey gathered from bees in the garden.

Andy Polaine, Offenburg, 2026

THE PARADOX AT THE HEART OF THE HUMAN FUTURE

On the afternoon of 13 March 2016, in a conference room at the Four Seasons Hotel in Seoul, a man sat across from a machine in a game of Go.

Lee Sedol was already down three games to none. The world's cameras were on him, broadcasting to more than 200 million viewers, and the story everyone was preparing to tell was simple: the machine had won. AlphaGo, built by a team at Google DeepMind, had taken all three, a result that stunned professional commentators and sent shockwaves through the global Go community. The match was played under Chinese rules, with two hours of main time for each player and three 60-second *byo-yomi* periods after that. Before the match began, Lee had told journalists he expected to win four games to one, or perhaps five to zero. He had been a professional since he was twelve, and was widely considered the finest player of his generation. The idea that a machine could beat him was, to many in the Go world, still faintly absurd.

Then came Game 2, and Move 37.

On its thirty-seventh move, AlphaGo placed a black stone on the fifth line, a shoulder hit no human professional would have considered. The commentators fell silent. Fan Hui, a European Go champion serving as an analyst, stared at the board and said later that it was not a human move, that he had never seen a human play it. AlphaGo's own probability estimates suggested the move had only a one-in-ten-thousand chance of being played by a human in that position.[1] But it worked. It worked brilliantly, reshaping the flow of the game in a way the commentators needed several minutes to see. Lee left the room after the game, visibly shaken. After Game 3, he apologised publicly, his voice tight with exhaustion and something close to grief. He told the press that he wanted to apologise first, that he should have shown a better result, and that he was sorry for not being able to satisfy so many people's expectations.

Game 4 should have been a formality. For three straight games the machine had played with what observers described as alien beauty. The match was already decided.

Seventy-eight moves in, Lee placed a white stone on the board: Move 78, a *tesuji* (a tactical sequence) the commentators could not immediately read. Some thought it was a mistake. Others fell silent, watching. What happened next would become one of the most studied moments in the history of artificial intelligence. AlphaGo's evaluation network misjudged the position. The machine that had played with such devastating elegance began to spiral. Its moves grew erratic, confused. Lee pressed the advantage with calm precision, and AlphaGo resigned.

Move 37 had been the machine's moment of apparent creativity, the alien beauty of a move no human would have played; Move 78 was the human's answer two games later. The machine had found its move by processing millions of games, surfacing a statistical pattern human intuition had never reached. Lee's move came from somewhere harder to locate, from the accumulated pressure of a lifetime sitting at a board and knowing that, in that moment, calculation was no longer enough.

Lee had won one game out of five, against a machine that would, by every measure, go on to prove unbeatable. When he retired from professional Go nearly four years later, he told reporters: "Even if I become the number one, there is an entity that cannot be defeated."[2]

AlphaGo won the match four games to one. In the years since, it is Lee's single victory people return to when they ask what it means to be human in the age of AI: Move 78, the move that came from a lifetime sitting at a board, from whatever happens inside a human mind when statistics run out and only reach is left.

The machine played with devastating elegance, and the world watched, and what the world remembered was the human who refused to stop trying.

I did not watch the match live. I came to the story the way most people did, in fragments and retellings, long after the result was settled. But the question the match left behind followed me through a series of careers and countries, eventually depositing me in a small town in south-eastern Australia with clay soil and an overgrown backyard. It was simple enough: if the machine can do the thing, why does it still matter that a person did it?

Around the time I started writing this book, I shipped a solution to a problem I'd spent days stuck on. The AI cracked it in twenty minutes. It was clean, and it worked, but when a colleague asked about a line in the fix, I paused. The answer was there. The path back to it was not.

I arrived here in Australia after nearly a decade of moving around the world. I began in New Zealand, where I was born and grew up, then went out to Australia, across to Mexico, through Southeast Asia and Europe and the Americas, looping back, and out again. Flight attending paid the way at first, then freelance copywriting and web development. I knew visa rules better than I knew almost anything else, and everything I owned fit into one bag.

My partner, our daughter, and I settled in Victoria in 2024, in a farming town outside Melbourne. Less than a year in, we bought a 1950s weatherboard house to renovate. Just as quickly as I'd slipped into the life of a long-term solo nomad, I had become a homeowner, a partner, and a parent. The backyard was barren when we arrived, just dried grass and clay soil, and an ancient apple tree dropping a little fruit for no one. When spring came, the ground started giving things back: Japanese anemones along the fence line, belladonna lilies pushing through where we had assumed nothing lived, all of them planted by someone who gardened this block many years ago and left no name behind. I have since added over a hundred varieties of my own.

We stopped here for our daughter. She was three months old when we landed, and the visa application had gone in almost as soon as she was born, because I wanted her near my family after a decade away. The garden started the same way the settling did: deliberately, and against my own momentum. I had spent eight years choosing the version of life where nothing needs watering. Then my daughter arrived. I picked the slow thing on purpose, knowing exactly what the fast thing felt like. This book is that choice, examined.

The longer I work with AI, the more I think of it as a mirror. It reflects back what you bring to it, and in that reflection you see yourself more clearly, including what you would fight to protect.

I have spent months writing this book with AI assistance, which is either the most ironic thing I have ever done or the most candid. An AI collaborator helped with research and structure, and asked me questions from my own life that unlocked things I did not know I had to say. Every sentence you read is one I wrote, and rewrote, and in some cases wrote a third time. The AI held the scaffolding steady, and I built. I am transparent about that collaboration throughout these pages.

Everything I have done for a living has shaped how I see the question at the centre of this book: what does it mean to create something as a human, when a machine can do it faster? Each role taught me what it feels like to work with your hands, your instincts, your whole attention. Those feelings are the lens I have written this book through.

My father was a software developer and computing lecturer. He died before AI became what it is now. He taught me things I am still catching up to. My mother is an artist who has never seen technology as the enemy of making; she makes prints and sketches, and builds worlds in virtual reality. She moves between them without apology, because for her the question has never been which tool is more legitimate but what she is trying to make and what will get her there.

Lee Sedol lost the match, and found something in the losing that no victory could have given him: a clarity about what the game had meant to him beyond winning. That clarity is what this book is for.

You might not agree with everything in here. I'd be a bit surprised if you did, actually. Some of what I argue is deliberately one-sided, because I'm more interested in what it makes you think than in being right about it. The Conversation Starters at the end of each chapter are especially for the moments when you want to push back. And if you want something more hands-on, the Appendix at the back has practical exercises tailored to your specific creative discipline.

Now, sit back, relax, and let me tell you something about Pokémon cheat codes.

Conversation Starter "What do you use AI for, and what have you found yourself craving more of lately?"

PART I

THE HUMAN SOUL IN AN AGE OF GENERATION

1

THE VOID OF EARNED-NESS

When I was a kid, I was pretty into Pokémon. I had the playing cards, the Game Boy games, and the ROMs that let me play them on my computer. The premise was simple: explore the world collecting strange little creatures, each one rarer than the last. But one place changed the rules, a kind of digital wildlife reserve tucked inside the game called the Safari Zone.

In the Safari Zone you didn't battle Pokémon the way you normally would. You wandered through tall grass with a limited number of steps, throwing Safari Balls and hoping the creature wouldn't bolt before you could catch it. Some of the rarest Pokémon in the game lived there, but the odds of encountering them were terrible. Most of the time you just walked, and walked, and waited.

Sometimes, after minutes of wandering, a rare one would finally appear. Your heart would jump. You'd throw a ball and hold your breath, and the screen would flash with the message that crushed every kid who played those games:

The Pokémon fled!

PA: Ding-dong! Your Safari Game is over!

I would spend hours there anyway, and when the reward finally came it produced a feeling I can still remember nearly thirty years later: a burst of triumph that started somewhere behind my ribs and spread outward until my whole body felt warm. Once I discovered cheat codes, I could have any Pokémon I wanted: input a code and there it was. The rush was incredible at first, my Pokédex filling with rare after rare. The legendaries that had taken weeks of patient pacing now appeared with a few keystrokes.

It wasn't long after that I stopped playing.

The rarity was gone, because I could have anything without work. Whatever had been pulling me to play, that magnetic force that made me choose a Game Boy over television, over homework, over everything, it did not feel the same anymore. The collection was complete, and it was worthless. I did not understand any of this at the time, being a kid with no framework for why a game had stopped being fun. But what I was experiencing has a name, at least the one I give it: the void of earned-ness, that empty feeling when a reward that should have required effort arrives instantly, when you skip the work and arrive at the destination empty-handed.

Many years and several careers later, I discovered AI writing tools. Blog posts appeared in seconds, titles like "Five Things to Do in London" and "Best Restaurants in Barcelona" materialising fully formed before I had finished my coffee. I was travel blogging at the time, and I thought I had found an edge: nobody in my circles was using this yet. The impulse was the same one from Pokémon, that collector's urge to fill the Pokédex, fill the content library. At first it was intoxicating.

It felt like a drug, and the dopamine hit was real. Each new blog post appearing on my screen in seconds gave me that same surge of acquisition, the thrill of having something I did not have a moment before. I made dozens of them, hundreds of words pouring out in minutes: travel guides, restaurant round-ups, neighbourhood walks, all of it fluent and competent and perfectly structured.

But when I tried to edit them, to polish them and make them sound like me, I could not engage. Editing AI text felt like more work than writing from scratch, because the words were not mine and the observations were generic. The voice was a bland approximation of travel writing, competent and forgettable. Nothing in them held: no rough edge where my own thinking had snagged, no sentence that surprised me with where it went. So I ended up with a vault of junk, dozens of bad blog posts I will never use, never publish, never look at again. Every day that passes, they are more clearly crap, sitting in a dusty, untouched corner of my cloud drive. Instant creation felt amazing, but it had done exactly what cheat codes do: produced the destination without the work, and left me with a full vault and that same emptiness.

What happened when the cheat code arrived has a name in neuroscience, though I didn't know it then: the reward came with no prediction error, and the dopamine system does not fire for a reward it saw coming.

Earned-ness is the psychological weight a creation carries when you have worked for it, when you have used your body, spent time, risked failure, and overcome friction. The effort becomes part of the value, not separate from it. And the research on this is extensive.

In 2018, psychologist Michael Inzlicht and his colleagues began studying what they would call the effort paradox.[1] Their finding did not fit the standard economic model of human behaviour: we dread effort in anticipation, avoiding it, procrastinating, choosing the path of least resistance whenever we can, but once the effort is spent it makes the outcome feel more rewarding. We love having done hard things: the marathon medal displayed on the wall, the story of the difficult hike retold at every dinner party, the wobbly bookshelf we built ourselves somehow more cherished than any piece of furniture that arrived already assembled.

The paradox is that what we avoid, the struggle, the friction, is what creates the value. Remove it and you remove the reward, which is exactly what the cheat code does: it bypasses the process that made the Pokémon worth catching.

Years before Inzlicht published his work on the effort paradox, Michael Norton and his colleagues at Harvard had already noticed a related phenomenon in their lab.[2] The experiment was deceptively simple. They gave each participant an unassembled IKEA storage box, plain flat-pack cardboard with folding instructions, and asked them to build it.

Picture the scene: a university lab, fluorescent lighting, participants hunched over sheets of cardboard, squinting at wordless diagrams that could mean almost anything. The instructions were standard IKEA fare, those minimalist line drawings of a faceless figure performing steps that seem obvious only after you have already figured out what to do. People fumbled with tabs and folds, some getting frustrated, some having to start over. The boxes that emerged were, by any objective standard, not impressive: cardboard containers, some of them wobbling, some creased in the wrong places where someone had folded before reading ahead.

Then the researchers asked them all, "How much is this worth to you?"

The answer, consistently, was more than participants would pay for an identical, professionally assembled version. Even when the result was objectively worse, when the box was lopsided, when the folds were uneven, the builders valued it more. Norton and his team called it the IKEA effect: the investment of labour creates a kind of love in which the process counts for more than the result.

What struck the researchers was how irrational the effect appeared on the surface. A wonky box is worth less by any measure a market would recognise. But the participants weren't valuing the box, they were valuing the experience of having built it, the memory of their own hands folding the cardboard, the mild frustration of the instructions, the satisfaction of the final click. They would pay significantly more for what they had struggled to make than for the identical object someone else had made perfectly. The effort had become inseparable from what the object was worth to them.

In 2023, Yunhao Zhang and Renée Richardson Gosline at MIT designed an experiment to test a question marketers and technologists had been arguing about without much evidence: whether people respond differently to content based on who made it, or whether quality alone determines their judgement. They had marketing copy and persuasive content produced four ways (by professionals only, by AI only, by humans then AI, and by AI then humans) and asked hundreds of evaluators to rate it. When evaluators had no information about the source, they rated AI-generated content higher on average. The machine-made copy was judged more persuasive, more polished: on blind taste, the machine won.

But the experiment did not stop there. When a second group evaluated the same content knowing which method had produced each piece, the ratings for any content involving a human rose. The human-only content climbed significantly. The AI-only content did not drop (readers did not punish the machine for being a machine) but the human work gained value that quality alone had not given it. This was not simply a preference for the human-made. It was a revaluation, one that had nothing to do with what the content was doing and everything to do with what the content represented: that a real person had spent real time with the brief, had wrestled with it, and had put their name on the result.

The same revaluation is playing out, at civilisational scale, in the music industry.

In 2022, vinyl records outsold CDs in the United States for the first time since 1987: 41 million vinyl albums sold versus 33 million CDs, according to the Recording Industry Association of America.[3] By 2023, vinyl had grown to 43 million records, generating 1.4 billion dollars in revenue, marking the seventeenth consecutive year of growth.

In an era when you can stream any song ever recorded, instantly, for free or nearly free, people are paying thirty dollars for a single album pressed onto a heavy, scratchable disc that requires a dedicated machine to play.

Audiophiles will argue the sound quality question endlessly, but the data suggests most buyers are not audiophiles, and the format is famously inconvenient. Earned-ness is not the only explanation for vinyl's revival, but it is one of them. You choose the record, carry it home, handle it carefully, sit down and give it your whole attention. The experience asks for your body and your time, and in return gives you what streaming cannot: the feeling that you participated in the listening, that the music didn't wash over you but that you went to meet it.

Of course, the convenience of streaming democratised music access in a way vinyl never could. But the trade cost a different kind of value.

Years before anyone worried about machines writing essays, a psychologist at Columbia University noticed a change in how her students remembered. Betsy Sparrow, working with Jenny Liu and Daniel Wegner, designed a series of experiments that seem almost quaint now. Participants typed trivia statements into a computer, small facts of the kind that used to win pub quizzes, like an ostrich's eye being bigger than its brain. Half were told the computer would save what they typed. The other half were told it would be erased.

The people who believed the computer would remember for them did not bother remembering for themselves. Their recall of the facts was measurably worse, and the effect ran deeper than laziness, because in a later experiment participants remembered which folder a fact had been saved into more reliably than they remembered the fact. The mind had made an accounting decision: the where was worth keeping, and the what could be let go.

Sparrow published the findings in Science in 2011 under the title Google Effects on Memory.[4]

Wegner had seen the pattern decades earlier, in couples. His research in the 1980s described what he called transactive memory, the way two people who share a life divide the work of remembering between them. One partner holds the finances and the car's service history, the other holds the birthdays and where the passports are, and together they function as a single memory system that neither could sustain alone.[5] It works beautifully, right up until it doesn't. Anyone who has watched a person lose a long-term partner knows that part of the grief is practical: half of the shared mind is gone, and the survivor discovers how much they had stopped carrying.

Sparrow's experiments showed that we had all, without ceremony or consent, entered a transactive memory partnership with the internet. The search engine became the partner who remembers everything, and we became the partner who remembers where to look.

I can feel the split in my own head. Whole regions of my work as a developer live permanently with the machine partner: regex patterns, snippets, URLs I have looked up fifty times and will look up a fifty-first. And then there are the plants. I have carried flower and plant names in my head since I was a small girl, hundreds of them now, an encyclopaedia I have never once thought to put down. Somewhere in between sit the phone numbers. I learned my partner's Australian number because I needed to, never his Mexican one, and my childhood landline is still in there, somehow, decades past any use for it.

Nobody mourns the lost skill of memorising epic poetry, and outsourcing the phone book to the phone freed room for better uses. Wegner himself thought transactive memory an achievement, not a failure. The couple that divides its remembering can hold more of a life between them than either could alone.

The effort of encoding is how the knowing becomes yours, and treating that effort as a cost to be minimised misreads what it buys. When I struggle a fact into memory, when I reach for it and miss and reach again, I am doing to knowledge what the Safari Zone did to Pokémon, making it scarce enough to be worth catching. The fact I can always look up sits in the same vault as my generated travel posts, technically mine, worth nothing to me.

Sparrow was measuring what the internet did to remembering over a decade before generative AI arrived to make the same offer about thinking. The pattern of the trade is identical, and each step of it feels sensible in the moment. We remembered where instead of what, and it seemed benign, because the what was always a search away. Now the machine offers to hold the argument itself, the structure, the phrasing, the connective thinking between one idea and the next, and we are deciding, mostly without noticing that we are deciding, which halves of the partnership to keep.

A dopamine system built over millions of years has opinions

about trades like this, and in the late 1980s a neuroscientist in Switzerland started measuring them.

The neurological story matters because it explains why the void is a physiological reality, not a moral failing or a nostalgic preference.

In the late 1980s and early 1990s, the neuroscientist Wolfram Schultz was threading electrodes into the brains of macaque monkeys at the University of Fribourg, recording the firing patterns of individual neurons as the animals received unexpected rewards. What he found surprised him: dopamine, the neurotransmitter most people associate with pleasure, does not respond to pleasure in the way we assume. It responds to prediction error, the gap between what you expected and what you got. When a surprise reward arrives, dopamine surges. When an expected reward arrives, even a pleasant one, dopamine barely moves. This is why the first bite of chocolate is always the best, and why an unexpected compliment lands harder than the same words said in a routine exchange. It is also why finding a twenty-dollar note on the ground feels like a lottery win while your regular salary barely registers.

The system is elegant and ruthless, designed to make you learn, not to make you feel good. Dopamine spikes encode surprise, telling your brain that the world has not behaved as predicted and the model needs updating. The bigger the gap between expectation and outcome, the bigger the spike. This is why the rare Pokémon, the one that appeared after hours of futile wandering, burned itself into my memory. The prediction error was enormous. Those hours had calibrated my expectation to zero, so when I finally caught it the dopamine surge was proportional to the gap, and the memory was sealed.

When I typed a cheat code and the Pokémon appeared instantly, no prediction error occurred, no gap opened between expected and received. The reward was flat. The dopamine system registered: predictable outcome, not interesting, move on.

AI does the same to creative work. When you ask AI to write a blog post and it produces one in seconds, the outcome is exactly what you expected, no gap between what you asked for and what arrived, nothing for the dopamine system to work with. Those AI-generated travel blog posts sat in my vault like trophies from a game I had stopped playing. Scrolling past them produced a faint irritation, not at the posts themselves but at the version of me who had thought they mattered. The writing was smooth and empty, each post a fluent approximation of what a real person might have observed. Nothing in them surprised me, because nothing in them had required me to wrestle with a sentence or stare out the window trying to find the right word, to discover halfway through a paragraph that what I was trying to say was not what I had thought I was trying to say.

The surprise of self-discovery, the prediction error of finding that your own mind contains what you did not know was there, is the deepest reward of creative work, and AI bypasses it entirely.

Csikszentmihalyi described what that reward looks like when conditions are right. He was a Hungarian-American psychologist who had survived the Second World War as a child and became preoccupied, in the aftermath, with a question he found almost nobody studying: what makes people absorbed in what they are doing? He began in the 1960s by interviewing chess players, rock climbers, surgeons, painters, factory workers, and musicians, asking them to describe the moments when their work felt most alive. One chess player told him that during a match several hours could pass that felt like minutes; a surgeon described forgetting hunger entirely during a complex operation. The accounts came from such different lives and converged so closely that Csikszentmihalyi suspected he had found something structural, not incidental.

People described a state of complete absorption in which self-consciousness dissolved and time distorted, where difficulty drove the work forward instead of stalling it. They spoke of working at the edge of their ability, using their full capacity without being overwhelmed by it, and feeling, paradoxically, as if the work were effortless even while it required everything they had. Csikszentmihalyi named this state "flow."[6] The word felt too simple for what the research kept showing, but it stuck, because the experience people were describing was simple: being fully in something, rather than partly in it while the rest of you wandered off.

The finding is structural: flow requires a precise relationship between challenge and skill. When a task is too easy relative to your ability, the result is boredom, the mind drifting off in search of something worth engaging with. Too much difficulty tips into anxiety, that sense of being overwhelmed without a foothold. Flow occurs in the narrow band between those two states, where the challenge is real and your skill is sufficient to meet it. Csikszentmihalyi called this the flow channel, and it shifts as you develop, because a challenge that produces flow at one level of skill produces boredom once that skill becomes automatic. This is why experts in any field describe having to push into increasingly difficult territory just to recover the quality of engagement they used to find at lower levels, and why learning something entirely new tends to feel more alive than exercising a mastered skill.

To study this more precisely than interviews alone allowed, Csikszentmihalyi developed what he called the Experience Sampling Method. Participants wore a pager that would beep at random intervals throughout the day, prompting them to record what they were doing and how they felt. Over decades and thousands of participants across different cultures and walks of life, this produced one of the most thorough datasets of ordinary human experience ever compiled, and the finding was counterintuitive: the moments people rated as most satisfying were not the moments of rest or leisure they had spent the rest of the week anticipating. They were moments of full engagement in something difficult enough to require all of their attention. People were, on average, measurably happier at work than in downtime, as long as the work demanded something of them.

What this means for creative work with AI took me a while to see, and then I could not stop seeing it.

When you ask AI to write a paragraph you were going to write yourself, you have not made your work easier, you have removed the task entirely. The challenge that would have produced engagement, the friction of reaching for the right word, the cognitive stretch of structuring an argument, the small discovery of realising mid-paragraph what you were trying to say, never arises. Flow has nothing to form around. You cannot enter a state of full absorption in work you have outsourced, any more than you can feel the satisfaction of a climb by watching someone else make it.

This is different from using tools that extend your capacity without replacing your contribution. A surgeon using the best available instruments is still performing the surgery, still required to exercise judgement at every turn. A composer using notation software is still composing; the tool handles the transcription while the thinking stays theirs. Where a tool crosses into outsourcing is the moment the difficulty disappears entirely, the moment the work no longer asks anything of you. At that point flow becomes structurally impossible, and the work produces output without the experience that would have made it feel like yours.

I want to be precise about the ADHD dimension of this, because it gets discussed in ways I find reductive. People with ADHD have a differently calibrated dopamine system, one that requires novelty and real difficulty to sustain attention. Routine tasks, predictable outcomes, work whose solution is clear before you start: these are neurologically hard in a way that is easy to misread, and the explanation people reach for (laziness, lack of discipline) misses what is happening, which is that the conditions for attention are not met. The same brain that cannot fill in a routine form without enormous effort can, given the right challenge, enter a state of hyperfocus so complete that hours pass unnoticed and hunger stops registering. Hyperfocus does not arrive on demand, and it cannot be manufactured by deciding to concentrate harder. It arrives when the conditions are right, and a challenge whose outcome you cannot predict is one of those conditions.

I know this from the inside. The tasks I cannot start are rarely the hard ones; they are the ones with nothing to catch on: formatting a document, answering a routine email, completing a piece of work whose shape is entirely clear before I begin. My brain is not refusing out of defiance, it cannot find the edge.

The tasks I lose myself in are the ones with real stakes and real uncertainty. A debugging problem I have not seen before, where I have to work out the cause from scratch, is the clearest example; writing works the same way when I do not know what I think before I begin. Under these conditions, six hours pass without my noticing the light has changed outside the window; it is not concentration so much as being fully somewhere.

When I used AI to generate those travel blog posts, I was not making my work easier. I was making it invisible to my own nervous system. The task ceased to exist as anything to engage with, and my brain, which invests only where there is engagement, did not invest. This is, for an ADHD brain, almost worse than producing nothing: I had the visible evidence of productivity without the felt experience of it. The Pokédex was full and I had stopped caring about Pokémon.

Csikszentmihalyi's framework makes the loss structural: remove the challenge and you remove one of the two ingredients the flow channel requires. The channel is the condition under which most creative and intellectual work achieves its deepest quality, and knowing where it exists in your own practice, and where AI use collapses it, is the most practical thing this research offers.

Instant creation resembles instant food: it fills the space and solves the immediate problem, and the satisfaction is thinner.

When I write a piece myself, struggling with the words, finding my way into a paragraph through three failed attempts before the fourth one clicks, the result carries a weight that AI-generated text does not. Whether my own writing is better or worse than what AI produces is not the question. The value is in having worked the thoughts through myself, in having discovered midway what I was trying to say, which generated text never allows.

I live in a beautiful part of the world where koalas live wild but are not easy to find. You have to know where to look, and you have to walk slowly, eyes up in the eucalyptus canopy, scanning for the shape of a koala's back against a branch. You might walk for an hour and see nothing. And then, sometimes, you look up and there it is, grey fur against grey bark, impossibly still, watching you with an expression that seems to contain the entire history of a continent.

The rarity makes it precious, and the koala itself is the same animal whether I see it in the wild or in a wildlife park, but everything that matters sits on one side of the comparison: the search, the time spent in the bush, the sun on my neck, the magpies singing their liquid song from the canopy, the uncertainty of whether today would be the day. The search is the value. I have not really seen an animal until I have seen a wild one, and that insistence on finding rather than being shown has taken me to jungles on three continents looking for animals I might never find. AI could show me a perfect koala photo or generate a realistic video of me standing in a eucalyptus forest with a koala sitting above me, and it would mean nothing, because my body was not there, my time was not spent, my feet did not walk the track, my eyes did not search the canopy. The prediction error, the gap between "I might not see one" and "there it is," is where the meaning is, and AI cannot replicate that gap because AI cannot replicate the risk of failure.

Inzlicht's later research found something even more striking: "We can learn to seek effort for its own sake."[7] Our relationship to difficulty is not fixed.

I think I learned this as a chef. The early months of training were brutal: standing for fourteen hours, burns on my forearms from the commercial baking oven trays, the relentless pace of service, where every second counts and nothing pauses. I dreaded the four a.m. alarm, and my body ached, and my feet swelled inside my shoes until the laces cut into my skin. The kitchen in summer was suffocating, with ovens running at full capacity, gas burners roaring, the extraction fan fighting a losing battle against the wall of hot air that hit you the moment you walked in. My hands blistered and the blisters burst and the skin underneath was raw and I kept working because everyone kept working, because that was the deal, because the food does not wait for your pain to subside.

I never learned to love the kitchen the way some chefs describe, that romantic pull toward the line. But I did learn to love what hard work felt like afterwards, the satisfaction of a body that has been used fully, which is different from the tiredness of a boring day in a way your muscles understand even if your mind cannot explain. And cooking itself has stayed with me long after I left the profession. I still make stock from scratch, still prefer the slow version of a meal over the fast one, and the hours I spend in my own kitchen still count in a way that convenience never does. The effort left a mark, and the mark became a preference I did not choose so much as discover.

I have felt the same shift with coding. The first months of learning were miserable, staring at error messages that might as well have been in Sumerian, feeling stupid and slow while my brain tried to build new pathways. And then one day a function worked, something I had written from scratch, and the satisfaction was disproportionate to the accomplishment. It was a simple function, but it was mine, earned through confusion and frustration and the patience that comes from not having any other option. The dread of effort, which we all feel, belongs to the anticipation, not the experience. And the experience, once it begins, can become something you seek out, because you have learned that the other side of effort is a satisfaction nothing else provides.

Nothing that comes instantly feels important. As a compass for navigating the relationship between humans and AI, that rule holds well enough. The void of earned-ness is a recognition that effort creates meaning in ways that convenience cannot, that the shortcut, however thrilling in the moment, leaves you looking at a picture of an animal you were shown rather than one you found.

When you use AI, what are you giving up, and is the trade worth making?

Sometimes it is worth making. I will gladly use a bouillon cube when I am tired and my family is hungry. I use AI when I need to format references or organise research. The shortcut has its place, but I know the difference. And once you have felt the void, that empty feeling of a reward you did not earn, you cannot unfeel it.

Earned-ness is not sentimentality. It is a measurable psychological weight that shortcuts cannot replicate. Once you have felt its absence (that flatness where satisfaction should be) you understand what is at stake as AI gets better at doing the work for us.

The vinyl buyers recognise this feeling, and so do the hikers and the people who built the shelf themselves, joints and all. And the young version of me, pacing the Safari Zone, the one who hadn't found the cheat codes yet, she knew it too.

Conversation Starter "If AI could give you any skill instantly, fully mastered, which skill would you refuse?"

2

IMPERFECTION IS THE SOUL

My daughter was two when she brought home a necklace from daycare. It was penne pasta painted in bright, uneven strokes of red; some pieces glittered, others were bare. Small, overconfident hands had threaded the whole thing onto a green pipe cleaner. It was lopsided and imperfect and, to me, unimaginably precious. If someone offered a professionally crafted version, symmetrical and expertly painted, I would refuse. I don't want just any pasta necklace; I want this one. It carries what a perfect one never could: proof of my daughter's hands. When I look at it now I picture her little concentrating face, the memory of the afternoon she made it oddly more vivid than the object itself.

The imperfections aren't flaws to me; they're the signal that a human made this. The wobble is hers, the mess is hers, and that's what makes it irreplaceable. If you want to know why some things are precious, look for the evidence that someone you love shaped them.

In 1937, a Dutch painter named Han van Meegeren unveiled what he claimed was a newly discovered masterpiece by Johannes Vermeer, the seventeenth-century Dutch master. The deception would run for a decade. Abraham Bredius, the most respected

Vermeer scholar alive, examined the painting, The Supper at Emmaus, and declared it genuine – "I am inclined to say, the masterpiece of Johannes Vermeer of Delft." The Boijmans Museum in Rotterdam purchased it for a vast sum and hung it in a place of honour.[1]

The motive is what makes the story stick. He was a technically gifted painter whose own work had been savaged by critics. The Dutch art establishment had dismissed him as derivative, old-fashioned, a competent craftsman with nothing to say. The rejection was crushing, and his response was revenge. He would paint a "Vermeer" so convincing that the same critics who had dismissed his own art would fall over themselves to praise it, and in praising it, prove their expertise a sham.

He spent years perfecting his technique. The challenge went beyond painting like Vermeer; he needed to fool the scientific tests that art historians used to detect forgeries. He developed a paint mixture using Bakelite, a newly invented synthetic resin, which, baked in an oven, hardened to mimic the crackling of centuries-old oil paint. He sourced seventeenth-century canvases, scraping away the original paintings to provide an authentic base. He studied Vermeer's pigments and brushwork until his compositional habits became second nature. The preparation was obsessive, the work of a man consumed by the need to prove the world wrong.

Over the following years, van Meegeren produced more "Vermeers," including *The Last Supper*. Critics praised them and collectors paid fortunes. One ended up in the personal collection of Hermann Göring, the Nazi Reichsmarschall, acquired through a dealer during the German occupation of the Netherlands.

The story might have ended there, except that the Second World War ended and the accounting began. When Allied forces traced Göring's art collection, the trail led back to van Meegeren, who was arrested and charged with collaboration with the enemy for selling a Dutch national treasure to a Nazi leader. The charge carried a potential death sentence. He faced execution for having sold the enemy something precious; his only defence was to confess that the precious thing was a lie.

No one believed him. The idea that this ageing alcoholic painter had fooled the greatest art experts in the world was preposterous on its face. So the court ordered a test: van Meegeren would paint another "Vermeer" under supervised conditions. In a house rented by the Dutch government, under police guard, watched by court-appointed witnesses, journalists, and sceptics, he set up his easel and began work on *Jesus Among the Doctors*. Over the next few weeks a "Vermeer" emerged from nothing in front of them, the same luminous technique and careful composition that had moved critics to tears. The demonstration settled it: the masterpieces were forgeries.[2]

The paintings did not change. Overnight, the same canvases that had been described as containing the luminous soul of Vermeer became worthless. The pigments were identical and the composition unchanged; even the brushwork was the same brushwork that had been praised as genius. But once the story behind them shifted, once the world knew that the hand behind them belonged to a bitter, vengeful forger and not to a seventeenth-century master, the experience of looking at them changed entirely.

The imperfection we value is not always visible in the object. Sometimes it lives in the story behind the object, in the knowledge that a real person, with their own history, made this. Van Meegeren's forgeries were technically flawless, and that was their problem. They were too perfect, too meticulously assembled to look like anything but what they were pretending to be. When the truth emerged, the perfection itself became the evidence of deception.

AI-generated perfection reminds me of this. The analogy does not rest on fraud or deception. What van Meegeren's forgeries and AI outputs share is an absence of original story: a perfection that carries no record of someone working through their own experience to make it.

In Kyoto, a woman named Mio Heki practises an art that is the philosophical opposite of van Meegeren's forgery. Heki is a *kintsugi* master and *urushi* lacquer artist, trained in the painstaking tradition of repairing broken pottery with lacquer mixed with powdered gold.[3] Where van Meegeren spent years learning to hide the evidence of his own hands, Heki has spent years learning to celebrate damage. A bowl arrives in her studio broken, sometimes shattered into dozens of pieces, and she reassembles it with seams of gold that make the cracks not just visible but luminous.

The training for *urushi* work alone takes years, and the material itself resists the unprepared. *Urushi* lacquer comes from the sap of the *urushi* tree, harvested by hand, each tree yielding only a small quantity each season. The raw sap is toxic, powerfully so. Contact with skin causes a severe allergic dermatitis, an angry, blistering rash that can spread across the hands and arms and take weeks to heal. Apprentices learn the material by working through the reaction, their hands swelling and cracking as their bodies build tolerance. It is an initiation written on the skin, and you cannot master *urushi* without first being hurt by it.

Each layer of lacquer must cure at precise humidity before the next can be added. Heki works in a *muro*, a humidity-controlled curing cabinet, checking the lacquer's surface by touch and by instinct developed over thousands of hours. A single repair can take months. She applies the gold powder in the final stages, dusting it onto the wet lacquer with a fine brush, each seam a different width and texture depending on the character of the break. Heki has described her philosophy in interviews with the Kyoto Journal: the repair is not about restoring the object to what it was before, it is about transforming it into something that could not exist without first being broken.[4]

No two *kintsugi* pieces are alike, because no two breaks are alike. The gold seams are unique to this crack, this history, these hands. The imperfection becomes the identity. AI can generate a thousand perfect bowls, but it cannot generate one that has been broken and mended by someone who loved it enough to fill the cracks with gold.

Kintsugi did not come from nowhere. Four centuries before Mio Heki learned to work *urushi*, a tea master in Japan built an aesthetic philosophy out of the deliberate rejection of perfection, and he built it in the most dangerous place imaginable: at the elbow of the man who ruled the country.

Sen no Rikyū was tea master to Toyotomi Hideyoshi, the warlord who unified Japan in the late sixteenth century. Tea, in that world, was politics. The tea room was where alliances were made and rank was performed, and the vessels used in the ceremony carried the significance that titles and land carried elsewhere. The most prized were *karamono*, imported Chinese wares: porcelain of impossible thinness, glazes of machine-like evenness centuries before machines, bowls whose symmetry announced that their owner could afford the best thing in the known world. A single celebrated tea caddy could be worth a castle. Warlords traded them as instruments of state.

Rikyū looked at all of that flawlessness and walked in the other direction. For his tea he commissioned bowls from Chōjirō, a Kyoto craftsman who made roof tiles. The bowls were shaped without a wheel, pressed and carved by hand, fired fast and lifted hot from the kiln. They came out dark, uneven, the walls thick, the surfaces holding the memory of fingers. This became *raku* ware, and Rikyū set it at the centre of the ceremony, in rooms he stripped back: smaller, dimmer, entered through a doorway so low that everyone, warlord or merchant, had to bow to come in.

The story everyone tells about Rikyū is the one about the morning glories. It is traditional, not documented, so hold it lightly. Hideyoshi heard that Rikyū's garden was in full flower and announced he would come to see it. When he arrived, every morning glory in the garden had been cut. Furious, he stooped through the low door of the tea room, and there in the alcove stood a single stem in a vase. One flower, because a hundred flowers are a spectacle and one flower is an encounter.

It would be easy to read the rough bowls as humility, or as making do. They were something sharper: arguments. A perfect Chinese bowl is complete; it needs nothing from you, and it offers you nowhere to enter. It is finished in both senses of the word. Chōjirō's bowls were unfinished in the second sense, deliberately open, and the drinker completed them. Your hands found the places where his hands had been. The glaze pooled differently on every bowl, so the one you were holding existed nowhere else in the world. The imperfection was the point, chosen by a man who had access to the most flawless objects on earth and set them aside.

This is why *kintsugi* could arise at all. A culture that prized the *karamono* ideal would see a cracked bowl as a failed bowl. The aesthetic Rikyū codified was *wabi-cha*, tea in the spirit of *wabi*, and it saw the crack as biography; within a few generations the repair had become the gold seam. Heki's months of lacquer work sit directly downstream of a sixteenth-century decision that a roof-tiler's thumbprints were worth more than porcelain.

I did my own small version of this in a thrift shop, choosing a chipped milk jug over every flawless option on offer; I just did not know the choice had a lineage.

Rikyū's aesthetic power grew until it pressed against Hideyoshi's political power, and in 1591 the warlord ordered his tea master to take his own life.[5] Historians still argue about the precise trigger. Nobody disputes that the most powerful person in Japan put a man to death, and that the instruments of his offence were, in some real measure, bowls. Rough, dark, hand-pressed bowls, and the unbearable suggestion carried inside them: that the value of a thing might have nothing to do with its perfection, and that no amount of power can buy what imperfection carries.

Four hundred years later we are having the argument again with different instruments, an endless supply of flawless surfaces on one side and the thumbprint on the other.

The same logic applies to sound. Keith Jarrett's Köln Concert is one of the clearest examples I know of imperfection creating something unrepeatable.

In January 1975, Jarrett arrived at the Cologne Opera House to perform a solo concert and discovered the wrong piano waiting for him. It was a Bösendorfer baby grand, small and tinny, with sticky keys, weak upper registers, and pedals that did not work properly. It had been meant for rehearsals, not for a performance in front of fourteen hundred people. Jarrett's producer, Manfred Eicher, later said that Jarrett nearly refused to play. He was exhausted from a long drive, had barely slept, was wearing a back brace for chronic pain, and now the most basic requirement for a solo piano concert, a functioning piano, had been botched. Vera Brandes, the eighteen-year-old organiser who had fought to book him and staked her reputation on the night, reportedly convinced him to go ahead.[6]

Jarrett walked onto the stage, sat down at the inadequate instrument, and played for over an hour. The recording was released as *The Köln Concert*, and it sold more than 3.5 million copies, making it the best-selling solo jazz album and the best-selling solo piano recording in history.[7]

The critical consensus, which Jarrett himself has acknowledged in interviews, is that the piano's limitations shaped the performance in ways a perfect instrument never would have. Because the upper registers were thin, Jarrett stayed largely in the lower and middle ranges, which gave the music its warm, rolling, almost hypnotic quality. The weak treble meant he couldn't rely on bright melodic runs in the higher octaves, so he developed repeating ostinato patterns in the left hand, vamp-like figures that built slowly and drew the audience into a kind of trance. The sticky keys forced him to play with more physical intensity just to get sound from the instrument, and you can hear that effort in the recording, a percussive weight that a lighter touch on a responsive Steinway would never have produced. He was fighting the piano, and the fight made the music.

A perfect Steinway grand, impeccably tuned and responsive to the lightest touch, would have given Jarrett everything he needed, and the result would have been a different concert entirely. Probably a good one, possibly a brilliant one, but not this one. The constraints of the broken instrument didn't diminish the performance; they redirected it into territory Jarrett would not have explored otherwise, and the warm lower registers that define the album's sound came entirely from the piano's failures, not from any intention of his.

The recording is worth listening to even if jazz is not your thing, because you can hear what limitation sounds like when someone refuses to let it stop them. Jarrett audibly stamps his foot, groaning and vocalising as he plays, his body fully invested in wrestling music from an instrument working against him. It is not a clean performance, and some passages feel almost aggressive in their physicality. I have listened to technically flawless piano recordings that left me feeling nothing at all, and then I have listened to the Köln Concert and felt it through my bones.

Musicians and producers could now use AI to generate a perfect solo piano performance, every note precisely placed, every dynamic shift calibrated, played on a flawless virtual Steinway with no sticky keys, no weak registers, no physical limitations at all. It would be technically superior to the Köln Concert in every measurable way, and no one would listen to it twice. What makes the Köln Concert irreplaceable is the same thing that makes a *kintsugi* bowl irreplaceable: the history of what went wrong, and the human who responded to it. The music Jarrett made that night came out of the instrument's failures, shaped by them and inseparable from them, and if you removed the limitations you would lose the art entirely.

When I think about what AI optimises away, this is what I mean. It would have given Jarrett a perfect piano, and erased the stuck keys, the weak treble, the aching back, the near-refusal to play, all the friction that made the concert what it was. The soul of that recording lives in everything that went wrong.

That's why, when it came time to find a milk jug, I didn't go to a department store.

I love a good cup of tea, and I was thrilled to be given a tea-for-one set for Christmas, a little teapot that stacks into a cup, sits on a saucer, bone china with colourful flowers all over. As a gardener and a flower lover, I found it a thoughtful gift. But something was missing: a milk jug to go with it. Online, options were everywhere, most priced from fifteen to fifty dollars, all glossy and new. Instead I found the one I love most in a thrift shop for three dollars, tucked between a faded sugar bowl and a chipped plate. It has a tiny chip on the rim, doesn't match my tea set, and was never as fancy as the ones online. But I love it more than anything I could have bought, and the feeling comes not from the price but from the story of how I found it and the sense that it had already lived a life before coming to sit on my table. I keep meaning to find a better-matched jug, or perhaps I mean that I keep deciding not to.

Every morning, I pour milk from it into my tea, and it feels alive. It lived before me and has a past I'll never know. The chip is its history, and I am not afraid of further damage because it already wears its scars openly. A perfect new one would arrive without a past, without proof it had lived. AI-produced content carries the same emptiness: made fast, made indistinct, leaving nothing behind that anyone would keep.

Amit Bhattacharjee, Alixandra Barasch, and Klaus Wertenbroch ran a series of experiments on how we judge other people's taste.[8] When someone's choices were uniformly excellent, observers rated the choices highly but trusted the person less; taste that perfect read as performance. A few imperfect choices flipped the judgement, because the flaws were evidence that the preferences were real. What drew people was the signal the imperfection carried, the sense that a person had been there, choosing for themselves rather than performing.

Start with the bluntest version of the question: what is the belief that a human made something worth, in dollars?

At the State University of New York at Oswego, two computer scientists named Johnathon Hall and Damian Schofield tested what happens when the labels are stripped away entirely. They paired AI-generated images (made with Midjourney) against human-made artworks, matched for medium, style, and subject matter, and asked participants to compare them aesthetically and then assign a dollar value to each. The aesthetic judgements were close: AI images were chosen often enough that several matchups were coin flips. On the surface, the machine was competitive.

But when Hall and Schofield looked at the prices participants assigned, a gap opened that the preference ratings had not predicted. People consistently valued the human-made works higher, by fifteen to twenty-five per cent on average, even though they could not identify which was which.[9] In the debriefing, participants who were told that some of their favourites had been AI-generated insisted it did not change their view that AI art has no heart or emotion behind it. They had just chosen it. They had just preferred it. And they still believed, in some deeper register, that it was worth less.

The valuation was already tilting before anyone consciously knew why. The human fingerprint did not need to be identified. It only needed to be present.

What draws us is the narrative of humanness behind the object, the knowledge that someone was there, that a consciousness touched this and left a trace. We want evidence of a choice someone made. What we are seeing is vulnerability. Brené Brown argues that vulnerability, the willingness to be seen in our imperfection, is what makes connection and belonging possible, even though it looks from the outside like exposure.[10] If vulnerability is what connects us to each other, then imperfection is the evidence of vulnerability. When we see a wobbly line or a cracked glaze, we're seeing someone who showed up without armour, who said, here, I made this thing, and whatever its flaws, it is mine.

AI can't be vulnerable because it has no self to risk exposing. It has no nervous system that trembles before putting work out into the world, and it doesn't lie awake wondering if what it made is good enough. Perhaps that's why its perfect outputs leave us feeling nothing: they carry no signal that someone was brave enough to try.

Think of the open mic night singer whose voice cracks on the high note of their own song, or the student reading their poem aloud for the first time, eyes down. That gap, between what they intended and what they could execute, is the tenderness. We are moved by the attempt, by the willingness to show up before you are ready, not by the performance itself. AI has no version of that hesitation. It doesn't wonder if this draft is good enough to share, because it has no stake in how the work lands. That permanent composure may be one of its deepest limitations.

In the children's book *The Velveteen Rabbit*, a stuffed toy becomes "real" by being loved so hard that his fur rubs off, his eyes lose their shine, and his shape changes from being squeezed too tight by small arms. The Skin Horse explains it to him: "It doesn't happen all at once. You become. It takes a long time. That's why it doesn't happen often to people who break easily, or have sharp edges, or who have to be carefully kept. Generally, by the time you are Real, most of your hair has been loved off, and your eyes drop out and you get loose in the joints and very shabby. But these things don't matter at all, because once you are Real you can't be ugly, except to people who don't understand."[11]

My daughter has a favourite toy, the one she drags everywhere, sleeps with, drops in the dirt, and demands at bedtime with increasing urgency. Its fur is matting in places and one ear is stiffer than the other from being gripped so many times. If someone showed me that toy in showroom condition, I would know it was not loved. The worn spots are the proof of care. AI generates the pristine bunny, the one that has never been dragged across a floor or pressed against a sleeping face, perfect and empty.

The same idea played out on a much larger scale one afternoon while I was hiking. I told you in the last chapter that I go looking for wild koalas instead of settling for shown ones. The park I was hiking through is home to the Strzelecki koala, a genetically distinct population found only in these ranges, smaller and darker than the koalas you see in zoos, and increasingly difficult to find. I was out to see if I could spot any, scanning the canopy at every pause in the trail. The path wound through stringybark eucalyptus-covered hills, then down into ferny gullies. Charcoal-black trunks rose between the trees, huge, monstrous pillars charred by bushfire, some hollowed out completely, standing like dark columns against the regrowth. Others had new growth sprouting from the base, bright green shoots pushing out of blackened bark, impossibly alive.

Wildfires are destructive, but they also play a regenerative role in the Australian ecosystem. Many native seeds need to be smoke-treated before they will germinate.[12] The seeds sit in the soil for years, decades sometimes, waiting for fire. Without it, they never become what they're meant to be. The burnt trees aren't damaged trees; they're trees that have been through fire, and they're still standing. The forest had been burning and regrowing for thousands of years before I walked through it, and it will keep doing so long after I am gone. Like *kintsugi*, but at the scale of an entire forest: the fire is the gold seam.[13]

I never did spot a Strzelecki koala that day, though I stopped and scanned the canopy a dozen times. As I walked, a huge monitor lizard, almost a metre long, sprinted across the path in front of me, and I stood with my heart going hard in my chest until it disappeared into the scrub. Nothing I could have planned for, nothing AI could have predicted or generated for me. It was a wild thing, in a wild place, and I was just lucky enough to be standing there when it happened. That surprise, the jolt of the unexpected, only comes from being in a real, imperfect, unscripted world. You do not get surprises in an artificial world, and you do not get humbled by monstrous black charcoal trees, because they would not carry the weight of a fire that actually burned something down.

So what am I saying when I say imperfection is the soul?

I'm saying the flaw is the feature that makes a creation human, the evidence of a nervous system at work, of time spent. It's the gold seam in the repaired bowl, the pasta necklace on the hook by the door, and in each case it's the story behind the object, the story van Meegeren faked and Mio Heki honours.

When AI makes perfect art, we feel the absence of this signal. The work is often impressive, but too smooth. Nothing in it says that someone sweated over a word choice at midnight, that someone's hand shook, that this cost anyone anything to make. It has no record of having tried and failed.

My daughter's pasta necklace will eventually fall apart, the wire will fray, the paint will chip, and the glitter will shed onto every surface it touches, as glitter does. When that happens, I'll probably put it in a box with her other precious things. None of them is perfect, yet all of them are irreplaceable.

AI's perfect outputs feel like a house staged for sale, fresh flowers on the table and nobody living there. Perfection implies a maker who left no trace. The things we keep are the ones where the maker couldn't hide, where the cost of making it shows. That gap between what was intended and what actually happened is the evidence that a real person was there. The evidence is what we keep.

Conversation Starter "If AI could produce a flawless version of your most treasured possession, would you swap it?"

3

CULTURAL VALUES AND AI RESISTANCE

In 1986, McDonald's opened a restaurant at the foot of the Spanish Steps in Rome.

The Piazza di Spagna is one of the most iconic public spaces in Europe; the baroque staircase spills down from the Trinità dei Monti church in a cascade of travertine, worn smooth by centuries of Roman feet. The bottom of the piazza opens out into a district where food has been bought and sold since before the Renaissance. Keats died in a house overlooking those steps, and generations of Roman families have gathered there on summer evenings, eating gelato, talking, and doing what Romans do better than anyone – turning the act of eating into the act of living. And now McDonald's had arrived at the exact base of those steps.

Carlo Petrini was a left-wing food writer and activist from the Piedmontese town of Bra, a small place in the Langhe hills known for its slow pace and its serious food. He was furious, and organised a protest at the site; the scene that followed became one of the founding myths of a global movement. Demonstrators gathered at the Piazza di Spagna, brandishing bowls of penne and plates of pasta, as if offering communion to the steps themselves. They chanted about what was being lost: the local food culture and regional culinary knowledge that could not survive a standardised menu applied identically everywhere on earth. The image was deliberately theatrical: here were Romans, in one of Rome's most sacred public spaces, eating the food their grandmothers made, in protest against a corporation that wanted to replace it with a hamburger wrapped in paper. The clash could not have been more vivid: a thousand years of culinary tradition on one side, and on the other a product optimised for speed and cost alone.[1]

Three years later, in 1989, the Italian journalist Folco Portinari drafted a manifesto, signed in Paris with Petrini among its signatories. "We are enslaved by speed," the manifesto declared. "Our defence should begin at the table." Delegates from fifteen countries signed. Each was committing to a philosophy that extended far beyond food, and to a fundamental question: what is worth doing slowly in a world that rewards doing everything fast? The movement Petrini founded, Slow Food, grew from that handful of signatories into a global organisation present in over 160 countries, with programmes protecting endangered food traditions, supporting small-scale farmers, and training a new generation to taste the difference between food that carries history and food that carries nothing but calories. Slow Food has not been without its critics; the movement has been accused of romanticising food traditions that are themselves exclusionary, available mainly to those with the income and the time to seek them out. Petrini has answered this, imperfectly, by pointing to the movement's support for small farmers in the global south.[2]

Petrini's rage was about what the burger represented, not the burger itself. It was the idea that a thousand years of Roman food culture, the grandmothers who taught their daughters to roll pasta by hand, the neighbourhood trattorias where the menu changed with the season because the ingredients came from the farm down the road, the regional variations in a single dish that could tell you within fifty kilometres where you were in Italy, could all be replaced by a standardised product, optimised for speed and cost and nothing else. The food was not the issue; Petrini was mourning everything the food had been part of. I think about Petrini sometimes when I use AI tools.

The output is usually fine, and the speed is remarkable, but I wonder what gets lost in the process.

Vinyl records, as we saw, are outselling CDs at a moment when streaming is cheaper and more convenient than it has ever been. Etsy keeps growing; handwriting classes are filling up as voice-to-text becomes ubiquitous. A pattern runs through all of it: a reaching back toward the evidence of human hands.

The maker economy is growing, and it is growing fastest in the demographics that use technology most. Young people who grew up with smartphones and social media are signing up for pottery classes, learning to knit, buying handmade goods at premium prices. Many of them use CNC machines, laser cutters, and 3D printers, because the technology was never the issue. What people are reaching for is evidence of a human on the other end, the slight unevenness of a hand-thrown pot or the knowledge that someone spent time making this exact thing for someone like them. The growth of maker culture tracks almost exactly with the growth of digital culture. People who spend their days consuming online content seem to want physical objects they can touch. The timing is not coincidental, I suspect: when the human system is flooded with that kind of input, it begins to crave something it can hold in its hands. In New Zealand, we have an affectionate name for this: the Number 8 wire mentality, after a gauge of fencing wire that has become legendary for its versatility. Kiwis use it to fix everything: cars, farm equipment, furniture, anything that breaks. It became a symbol of national character, one that preferred making and fixing to buying and replacing. Growing up there, I remember things being fixed instead of replaced, friends and family and neighbours finding new uses for old objects, treating everything as if it had a future beyond its current form. It was a set of values so deeply embedded in the culture that nobody needed to articulate them, and it was never about whether you had the money, either – the assumption was that things were meant to last, and that the process of fixing taught you something buying new never would.

So, I wonder: is my resistance to AI-generated content culturally determined? I value both progress and tradition deeply, and I live in the tension between them every day. That tension is productive, I think, but my blend of comfort and discomfort with AI is not universal; it is the response my culture taught me to have, not the objectively correct response to the technology.

In 2003, on the other side of the world from where I was growing up, a Cal Poly San Luis Obispo student named Kyle Wiens broke his iBook G3 laptop and went looking for a repair manual.[3] He could not find one anywhere: not at the Apple store, not online, not from any third-party source. Apple did not publish repair documentation for consumers. Their position was that broken devices should not be repaired but returned directly to Apple or replaced entirely. The message was clear: you were permitted to use the object, but understanding how it worked was not part of the deal. The hardware enforced it, and the enforcement tightened over the years that followed. Apple began using proprietary pentalobe screws, a five-pointed design that no standard screwdriver could open, specifically to prevent customers from getting inside their own machines. Batteries were glued in place, components were soldered to boards where they had previously been modular, and every design choice pointed in one direction: this device was not built to be fixed.

Wiens wrote his own repair guide and published it online, then another, and then he and a fellow student, Luke Soules, built a website called iFixit, where anyone could find step-by-step instructions for fixing their own electronics. What began as one student's irritation at not being allowed to fix something he owned became a global movement, and by the 2020s, iFixit had grown to around 140 employees in the United States and roughly 70 more in a European subsidiary based in Stuttgart. They had published thousands of free repair guides and become the most visible face of the right-to-repair movement worldwide. iFixit's teardowns of new products on launch day became public accountability rituals, shaping how the tech press evaluated new hardware; when iFixit gave a product a low repairability score, it made headlines, and manufacturers noticed. Wiens testified before legislatures, sparred publicly with Apple over glued-in batteries and proprietary screws, and framed the entire fight in language any Kiwi would recognise: "Access to the knowledge of how to repair things is a fundamental human right."[4] In 2021, President Biden signed an executive order urging the Federal Trade Commission to support consumers' right to repair their own devices. The European Commission announced plans for EU-wide right-to-repair legislation. France introduced a repairability index, a policy requiring manufacturers to rate how repairable their products were on a scale displayed at the point of sale, so that consumers could see, before buying, whether a laptop or a washing machine was designed to be fixed or designed to be thrown away. By early 2025, right-to-repair bills had been introduced in every US state.

"This is more than a legislative landmark – it's a tipping point. We've gone from a handful of passionate advocates to a nationwide call for repair autonomy," Wiens said. "People are fed up with disposable products and locked-down devices. Repair is the future, and this moment proves it."[5]

AI-generated content is the ultimate replacement-culture product: you generate it rather than writing it yourself, outsourcing the skill and banking the saved time for something else. The right-to-repair movement insisted that the doing itself is the point, that the time spent understanding how something works is not a cost you subtract from the outcome but part of the value you take away from it. Wiens was fighting for a particular relationship between people and the things they use, one in which that understanding is part of what it means to own something. But his battle is not unique – he has a historical predecessor in William Morris.

In 1851, William Morris visited the Great Exhibition at the Crystal Palace in London and was horrified.[6] The exhibition was meant to showcase the triumphs of industrial production, but Morris, then a young man who would become one of the most influential designers in English history, saw only ugliness: mass-produced goods stamped out by machines and stripped of the craft and care that had defined making for centuries. Everything was technically competent, but Morris found it spiritually inert.

Morris's response was to build the alternative. In 1861, he founded

Morris, Marshall, Faulkner & Co. (later simplified to Morris & Co.), a workshop that produced handmade wallpapers, textiles, stained glass, and furniture. But Morris did not oversee the work from a distance; he insisted on learning every craft himself before he would allow his workshops to produce it. He taught himself to weave on a loom he had installed in his bedroom, and spent months experimenting with natural pigments, chasing colours the industrial dye works could not match. He learned hand printing and typesetting before he considered himself qualified to oversee them. Every product that left Morris & Co. was designed by a man who understood the craft from the inside, whose hands knew what the material could do because he had done it himself first. His wallpapers, those intricate, flowing patterns of Willow and Acanthus and Strawberry Thief, are still in production more than 150 years later, a tribute to the depth of knowledge embedded in them as much as to their beauty. His philosophy was radical in its simplicity: "Have nothing in your houses that you do not know to be useful, or believe to be beautiful."[7] In his 1880 lecture "The Beauty of Life," delivered to the Birmingham Society of Arts, Morris went further. "The cause of art is the cause of the people," he declared, arguing that beauty was everyone's right, not a privilege confined to the wealthy, and that industrial production was destroying it. In his 1884 lecture "Useful Work versus Useless Toil," he drew a line that reads as though it were written about the AI era. Industrialisation was destroying meaningful work, he argued, because of the way machines were being used: they severed the connection between the maker and the made. The factory worker produced objects but had no relationship with them, no pride in them, and no stake in how they turned out. The objects were technically adequate, but nothing human had been put into them, and you could tell. Morris knew the irony and struggled with it: the objects his workshops produced, beautiful as they were, were affordable only to the wealthy. The socialist who believed beauty was a right for everyone built a business whose customers were the ruling class. His designs have since become some of the most mass-reproduced patterns in the world: the Strawberry Thief on a cushion cover from a chain store, the Acanthus on wallpaper printed by the roll. A posthumous irony, perhaps.[8]

The Arts and Crafts movement Morris inspired was, in effect, a contract with industrial technology, defining the terms under which we use machines. We will use them where they serve human flourishing, and we will refuse them where they diminish the maker's relationship with the work. The contract kept technology in a subordinate position. The movement spread across England and then across the Atlantic, inspiring guilds of craftspeople committed to handmade production, from furniture makers in the Cotswolds to potters in the Lake District, who saw their work as resistance to a vision of progress that valued output over meaning. In America, Gustav Stickley and the Roycrofters built communities around the same principles, and the influence rippled through architecture, typography, and interior design for generations. Morris did not stop a single factory, but he named a feeling that millions of people shared and gave them a framework for acting on it, insisting that machines serve human purposes rather than the other way around.

I hear Morris's voice in Petrini's manifesto and in Wiens's testimony, and I hear it in the Number 8 wire mentality I grew up with. Separated by culture and by more than a century, they kept arriving at the same insistence: the making carries the meaning.

These values are not equally available to everyone. Choosing repair over replacement, or buying handmade instead of mass-produced, costs more and takes more time; that is a luxury many people cannot afford. Many people use AI-generated content because they cannot afford the human alternative, and buy mass-produced goods because craft costs more, and neither is a failure of values. Cultural values cannot exist in an economic vacuum, and to romanticise craft without acknowledging its cost would be dishonest. The origin of the Number 8 wire mentality is clarifying, though: it emerged from economic necessity. People fixed things because they could not afford to replace them. The reverence I feel for repair is inseparable from the reality that, for earlier generations of New Zealanders, there was no choice: replacement was not available.

In Japanese culture, the concept of *mottainai* expresses regret over waste, a recognition that objects have value beyond their utility, that the energy, materials, and labour that went into making them deserve to be honoured by using them fully. It carries spiritual weight, rooted in Buddhist philosophy, and it shapes everything from how food is eaten to how old garments are mended and repurposed. Alongside it sits *shokunin*, the artisan spirit. In a culture that holds these values, AI-generated craft would feel like a violation of the process itself, something closer to sacrilege than convenience.

Friends in Sweden bring the same measured sensibility to AI tools, *lagom*, just the right amount: picked up when useful, set aside without ceremony.

In Teotitlán del Valle, outside Oaxaca City, a weaving family showed me where their all-natural rug dyes came from, insects and petals and rinds, and how the yarn was rinsed down at the town river. A single rug can take months, or even years. Machine-made copies of Zapotec patterns exist now, and to most eyes the difference barely registers. I wanted a real one that day; alas, I was a nomad, with no home to send it to.

Everything I have described so far leans one way. Petrini with his penne, Wiens with his screwdriver, the *mottainai* sensibility, my own Number 8 wire wiring: these are all cultures of resistance, and if I stopped here you could be forgiven for concluding that depth always votes against the machine. So I want to tell you about the country that refuses my frame entirely.

One Korean phrase reaches you within hours of arriving in Seoul: *ppalli ppalli*. Hurry, hurry. People use it with affection and with exasperation, usually both at once, and it describes how the country runs. Food arrives faster than seems physically possible. Broadband was world-leading while other countries were still dialling up. When something new works, Korea does not adopt it so much as absorb it at full speed.

Generative AI met *ppalli ppalli* and the result was predictable. Through 2025, South Korea recorded the fastest growth in generative AI use in the world, with usage climbing by around eighty per cent in a single year, and became the second-largest market for ChatGPT subscriptions on earth, behind only the United States.[9] The moment that tipped it into the mainstream was not a productivity tool. In April 2025, Ghibli-style portraits generated with ChatGPT went viral across Korean social platforms, and millions of people used AI for the first time to make something whimsical for their friends. Nobody was optimising anything; they were playing.

My resistance-shaped lens expects to find shallowness alongside that: disposability, a culture that has traded its crafts for speed. Instead, Korea has run a formal system for protecting craft mastery since 1962, designating individual artisans as holders of Important Intangible Cultural Properties, the people commonly called living national treasures. Goryeo celadon, with its impossible jade-coloured glaze, is still made by masters whose lineages the state documents and funds. *Hanji*, the mulberry-bark paper that survives for a thousand years, is still beaten and floated by hand. *Kimjang*, the communal making of kimchi, is inscribed by UNESCO as intangible cultural heritage, and families still do it together every winter, not as a museum re-enactment.[10]

The same culture, the same people, often the same person. A Seoul office worker who generated a Ghibli portrait of her grandmother in April may spend a Sunday in November elbow-deep in seasoned cabbage with that grandmother, and she would be puzzled to hear that the two are in tension, because in her week they never meet as rivals. The either-or that structures this chapter, resistance here and embrace there, is itself a cultural artefact.

I spent a week in Seoul on a work trip in 2022, and what I brought home was the contrast: both speeds running side by side through the same streets, a city untroubled by the combination. All of it surprised me. My own frame still treats the two as rivals; I have stood in a place where they are not.

One more turn brings the book's opening image home. Lee Sedol is Korean. The match that gave this book its beginning, Move 37 and Move 78 and a man apologising to a country, happened in Seoul, and was felt there as something close to a national wound. Koreans wept over that match. And then the same country adopted the technology that beat him faster than almost anyone else on earth, while continuing to fund masters who spend fifty years on celadon glaze. If that seems like a contradiction, the contradiction is in the expectation. Nothing in the grief required refusal, and nothing in the adoption required forgetting. The country that loved Lee Sedol enough to mourn him understood, perhaps better than the cultures that resist, what he meant when he said there is an entity that cannot be defeated: the machine had changed what winning meant, and it had changed nothing about why you sit down at the board.

Naming your cultural grammar gives you a bias you can examine rather than simply act on. Korea is the examination. My discomfort with AI is real, and the limitation it detects is real, and a whole civilisation is out there demonstrating that you can move at machine speed on Monday and kneel at the kiln on Sunday without splitting in half. Both of those facts get a vote.

These modern movements of resistance echo a much older, deeper form of knowledge, one where the connection between human practice and environment was a necessity measured in millennia, not a lifestyle choice. Aboriginal Australians have occupied this continent for over 65,000 years. For most of that time, and in many places still, they practised a form of land management that European colonisers took centuries even to begin to understand. The common term is "firestick farming," though that phrase, coined by the archaeologist Rhys Jones in 1969, flattens something far more complex into a label that sounds like a technique.[11] What Jones called a technique was closer to a relationship with Country, held in bodies and in stories, passed between generations through songlines, ceremony, and the patient act of walking with elders who knew which parts of the land needed fire and when.

Different plant communities required fire at different intervals, and the timing depended on wind, soil moisture, the behaviour of particular animal species, and the flowering cycles of particular plants in particular places. An elder burning Country in the Western Desert was not applying the same method as an elder burning

Country in the tropical north, or in the wet forests of Gippsland where I live now. The knowledge was local down to the level of individual ridges and creek systems, learned through observation over millennia and carried in memory, not in text. Victor Steffensen, a Tagalaka man and cultural burning practitioner, describes it in terms that make the complexity vivid: you read the country the way you read a face, and you respond to what it tells you it needs.[12] A burn conducted at the wrong time or in the wrong conditions could destroy what careful fire would have renewed.

The word "read" in Steffensen's description implies a literacy that has no written form. The knowledge is legible only to people who have spent their lives in relationship with a specific stretch of Country, walking it across seasons, watching how it responds to rain and drought and fire, learning from people who watched it before them and from people who watched it before that, back through more generations than most cultures can count. It cannot be extracted or stored, because it is performed, alive only in the doing of it, and when the doing stops, it does not sit on a shelf waiting to be retrieved. It degrades, and the Country, unburned and unread, degrades alongside it.

When British colonisation disrupted Aboriginal land management practices from 1788 onward, the consequences were concrete and dire. Colonial authorities suppressed cultural burning across much of the continent, partly because they did not understand it and partly because it interfered with pastoral land use. The fuel loads that Aboriginal burning had kept low for thousands of years began to accumulate, and within decades the character of fire on the continent changed. What had been frequent, low-intensity, mosaic burning, patchy and seasonal, managed with intimate knowledge of local conditions, gave way to infrequent, catastrophic wildfire that destroyed everything in its path. The 2019–2020 Black Summer bushfires burned over 24 million hectares and killed or displaced an estimated three billion animals.[13] Those fires were driven by climate change and drought, but fire ecologists including Steffensen have argued, convincingly, that the removal of Aboriginal burning practices over two centuries made the land far more vulnerable to catastrophic fire than it had ever been under Indigenous management.

Earlier, I described walking through the Strzelecki Ranges past charcoal-black trunks standing amid green regrowth, huge pillars scorched by bushfire with new shoots pushing from the base. I wrote about how many Australian native seeds need smoke treatment before they will germinate, and how they sit in the soil for years waiting for fire. What I did not say then, because it belonged here, is that the fire those seeds evolved alongside was the managed fire of Aboriginal land stewardship, not the catastrophic wildfire of recent decades: small burns calibrated to the needs of specific ecosystems, conducted by people whose knowledge of those ecosystems had been refined across more than two thousand generations of continuous observation.

Aboriginal fire knowledge is, with uncommon clarity, a kind of knowing that cannot be automated. You cannot write it into a manual. Colonial land managers tried to codify burning regimes into schedules and prescriptions, fixed intervals and fixed hectarage, and the results were consistently poor. The knowledge is relational rather than procedural, dependent on reading conditions that change from day to day and place to place, on recognising patterns that only become visible after years of attentive presence on the same Country. An algorithm could process satellite imagery, moisture data, and wind speed, and it might produce a burn plan that looked reasonable on paper. But it would not know that this ridge burns differently after a dry winter than after a wet one, or that the wallabies move through that gully at this time of year and need the corridor left unburnt, or that the grasstrees on the north-facing slope are ready for fire but the ones fifty metres away on the south-facing slope are not. That knowledge lives in specific people, held in relationship with specific places, and when those people are removed from the land, or when the chain of transmission between generations is broken, the knowledge does not persist in any recoverable form.

It would be easy, in a book like this one, to use Indigenous knowledge as a metaphor and then move on. But that would flatten it. Aboriginal fire knowledge is an actual, functioning system of land management that sustained a continent for longer than any other documented human practice, and its disruption produced measurable ecological catastrophe within a remarkably short timeframe. The people who hold this knowledge are alive, many of them fighting for the right to burn Country again, and the scientific community is increasingly recognising that they were right all along. Steffensen's work with the National Indigenous Fire Workshop and various state land management agencies is one strand of a broader movement to restore cultural burning practices across Australia, though the process is slow and politically complicated, because the knowledge was never centralised and cannot be scaled the way colonial institutions prefer.[14] No database could have preserved it, because it was never separate from the act of walking Country and reading it, from burning it in the right way at the right time. The knowledge and the practice were the same thing, and separating them destroyed both.

Each of these traditions produces a different emotional response to AI, and none of them is wrong.

I work with people from all over the world, and their reactions to AI tools vary more consistently with cultural background than with technical expertise. A colleague in Japan brings a different sensibility to AI-generated design than a colleague in San Francisco, and a colleague in Amsterdam weighs sustainability and longevity in ways I would not have thought to. They are all seeing the same technology through different cultural windows. Awareness of our cultural positioning helps us make more honest choices. When I recognise that my discomfort with AI-generated content is partly cultural, I can hold that discomfort with more curiosity and less certainty, and I can ask: Is this a real limitation of AI that I am detecting, or is this my Number 8 wire upbringing talking? Often, the answer is both, since the limitation is real and my cultural lens makes me more sensitive to it.

We rarely notice the cultural values we stand on, which is what makes them so powerful. A colleague who grew up fixing things with her father feels the absence of human effort in AI-generated content, while a colleague from a startup culture feels mostly excitement at the same output. The technology is identical; the cultural grammar each person uses to make sense of it varies enormously. Naming the grammar gives you a bias you can examine against the evidence rather than simply act on.

I shop at the local farmers' market most weekends. The couple who makes the sourdough talks about their starter the way other people talk about their pets, with a mixture of pride and mild anxiety about its well-being. Their loaves have a crust that crackles when you tear it, and the crumb inside is open and sour and alive. The vendors who grow and sell the tomatoes can tell you which varieties do well in the region's clay soil, and which ones need more sun than our summers reliably provide. Buying from them means buying into the place I live: its climate, its seasons, this particular corner of Australia. This knowledge changes the experience of eating in the same way that knowing a couple I once met in China had been shaping *baozi* dough since before dawn changes the taste of what they served me. The gift of living between cultures is the awareness that your values are values rather than objective truths: the person sitting next to you might see the same AI-generated image and feel something completely different, and both of your reactions are real, both shaped by where you came from.

Petrini with his penne, Morris at his loom, Wiens with his screwdriver, the elder reading fire into the ridge; all of them were insisting, in different ways, on the same thing: that the process is not separable from the product, and that what you lose when you remove the human hand is meaning. I have come to think that the discomfort many people feel about AI-generated content is this insistence surfacing in them, shaped by their own culture's version of the argument. And across every culture I have described here, the same feeling keeps appearing, even when the vocabulary differs: a sense of something absent, something technically correct but not quite there.

Conversation Starter "How do you think the culture you grew up in shapes how you feel about AI?"

4

WHY AI FEELS HOLLOW (AND WHY THAT MATTERS)

In the early hours of 1 April 2017, my train pulled into Xi'an, a city in central China, famous for its terracotta warriors and for being the eastern starting point of the Silk Road for over 1,000 years. It was around five in the morning, the city still dark and only beginning to wake around me. Down a side street, I found a *baozi* shop selling fluffy steamed pork buns, the street-food speciality of the area. The store was tiny, with seating for about four people. The floor space was shared with the production benches, and the walls were papered in rose print. It felt cosy, lived in, if a little dated and cramped.

An old couple were inside, working at pillowy mounds of snow-white dough, their hands covered in flour. They had been at it for hours already, kneading and folding, shaping the dough into buns. Everything about them said they had done this every morning for years. I sat down. The *baozi* came filled with pork, deliciously oily, served with broth and a dipping sauce. I ate and watched them work, their flour-covered hands pressing and turning, the dough yielding under the weight of their expert fingers. They did not hurry, and the buns were not identical, each one carrying the slight variations that come from a hand and not a mould. The pork filling was rich, and the broth was one of the best things I have ever tasted.

Sitting in that tiny shop at five in the morning, with rose wallpaper peeling at the edges and an old couple kneading dough in front of me, I thought I could return here to eat every day for the rest of my life. It is still one of my favourite meals. The *baozi* were excellent, but so was plenty of food I have forgotten. What I have not forgotten is the couple, their flour-covered hands at dawn, the smallness of the room, the years of practice visible in every motion. The food and its context were a single thing, and the taste included the story.

In the years since, I've never found pork buns that good, and not from a lack of trying. AI could replicate that *baozi* recipe with mixing machines, kneading the dough to the same consistency and filling each bun with the same ratio of pork and fat, and the result would be technically perfect. But the bun would arrive without the couple, without the years of kneading at five in the morning and the flour-covered hands, without the story or the atmosphere. Whatever it tasted like, I am confident it would not taste the way that bun tasted to me, that early morning when I sat in the heart of ancient China and devoured bun after bun.

The knowledge of human effort changes an experience in the same way that knowing a story is true changes how you hear it. The information is not separate from the sensation; the two are woven together. Knowing that the couple had been shaping *baozi* since before dawn made the filling taste richer, and watching their flour-covered hands work the dough gave the buns a quality they would not otherwise have had. This is not a delusion, it is how perception works: tasting is not something the tongue does alone, it draws on everything we know. The absence of that quality is what haunts AI-generated content. Artificial sweeteners taste hollow. You know this, even if you cannot quite articulate why. The first sip is sweet, your taste buds light up, and your brain registers sugar. But then a depth is missing, a richness, something like the caramel warmth of real sugar dissolving slowly and leaving a trace on your tongue.

Your body knows it too, in ways you cannot consciously detect. When sweetness hits your tongue, your brain prepares for what should follow: glucose, real calories. Insulin is released in anticipation, your digestive system readying itself for fuel. And then nothing arrives. Your body is left holding the door open for a guest who never walks through, compensating later by holding onto extra sugar the next time you eat something real. This is what AI content feels like: the signal comes, and then nothing arrives to back it up.

Wolfram Schultz spent years measuring the reverse case too, with some precision: what happens in the brain when an expected reward fails to materialise. The dopamine response does not return to baseline but drops below it, the nervous system marking the gap between what was signalled and what arrived. That gap may be hollowness itself: the brain's notation for a reward that was promised and never came.

A sauce that has reduced for an hour has a depth it did not have at thirty minutes, and no amount of heat will compress the difference. You can get close, you can get something that looks right, but your mouth knows. The depth comes from time; compress the time and you lose it. Don't get me wrong, I lean on cooking shortcuts often, when I am tired and the priority is getting food on the table rather than winning a cooking competition. Convenience is not a moral failing, and speed is not a sin. But the shortcut and the slow version are not the same: one carries the evidence of time and care, the other the convenience of speed. And once your body has tasted the version that took all afternoon, you cannot unknow it. Your tongue has been educated, and it will measure everything against what it knows is possible.

I think this is what is happening with AI content on a cultural scale. We are all, slowly, getting educated. The more we encounter AI-generated text and images, the more refined our detection becomes. Our palates are improving because we have been around it long enough to learn what absence feels like.

Wine people have a word for what the *baozi* had, *terroir*. The claim underneath it is simple: the same grape, grown in two different places, makes two different wines, and no amount of technique can move the difference.

Take Pinot Noir, the most place-sensitive grape there is. Grow it on the limestone slopes of Burgundy and it makes one wine; grow the same clone, with the same methods, on the volcanic soils of Oregon's Willamette Valley and it makes another, recognisably a sibling and unmistakably not the same. The difference is the accumulated specificity of somewhere: the soil and what died in it, the angle of the slope to the sun, the fog that comes or doesn't, the two hundred vintages of local judgement about when to pick. French law takes this so seriously that it names wines after places rather than grapes. A Burgundy is Burgundy, expressed through a grape. One wine writer called the quality "somewhereness," which is both clumsy and right.[1]

You do not need to care about wine for this to matter, because *terroir* is only the most codified version of a lesson food keeps teaching anyone who tries to move it. It is why the *baozi* in Xi'an cannot be extracted from the shop with the rose wallpaper, and why the first strawberry tastes of the wait. Food is the proof that meaning is grown somewhere rather than assembled anywhere.

Mexico taught me this over and over. Street tacos do not survive the trip anywhere; whatever arrives on the plate in another country is a photograph of a taco. In Oaxaca, where I lived for a time, almost nothing that came off a *comal* could exist anywhere else, because the *comal* was the least of it: the corn, the hands, the courtyard, the morning. Moroccan food does the same refusing. Some meals are places, and they decline to travel.

AI-generated content is grape without *terroir*. That comes close to a technical description of what a large language model is, and I don't mean it as an insult. The text is grown nowhere. No weather happened to it. It has no vintage, no slope, no two hundred years of local mistakes pressed into its habits, and when you read it, what you feel is the absence of somewhereness, the same emptiness you would taste in a wine engineered to be from nowhere, competent and balanced and homeless. I have been calling this hollowness. A wine-maker would say the wine has no *terroir*, and would mean the same: nothing happened here, nowhere, to no one, and you can taste it.

In the early 1990s, a cognitive psychologist named Elizabeth Loftus was working at the University of Washington, and she had been thinking about memory for years.[2] Her earlier research on eyewitness testimony had already unsettled the legal profession. Loftus had shown that the questions you ask a witness can alter what they remember; asking "How fast were the cars going when they smashed into each other?" produced higher speed estimates than asking "How fast were the cars going when they hit each other?" The verb changed the memory. But Loftus wanted to push further, to find out whether you could implant from nothing a memory of an event that had never happened, so she designed an experiment built on a lie about a shopping mall.

Loftus and her student, Jacqueline Pickrell, recruited participants and gave each a booklet containing four childhood stories. Three of the stories were true, and had been provided by a family member whom the participant trusted; the fourth was fabricated: a detailed account of being lost in a shopping mall as a child, around age five or six, separated from a parent, frightened and crying, eventually rescued by an elderly stranger who reunited them with their family. It had never happened, and the family member had confirmed as much. But it was plausible, the kind of ordinary childhood scare that could have happened to anyone, and it was presented alongside three real memories as though it were just as true.[3]

The participants took their booklets home. Over multiple follow-up interviews, spaced days apart, they were asked to recall as much as they could about each event. About a quarter of participants came to remember the fabricated event as real, not vaguely but in rich, specific detail. They added sensory details the researchers had never provided. Some became emotional while recounting it. They did not just accept the memory; they furnished it with the texture of lived experience, building a past that had never existed from the materials of their own minds.

Loftus's finding was unsettling, but what struck me was the

creativity of memory rather than its vulnerability. These participants were not being deceived in the ordinary sense; they were constructing. Their minds, given a scaffold, a plausible story from a trusted source, generated the experience to match. They supplied the colour, the feeling, and the physical weight of the moment, making the false memory real by filling it with their own lives. Loftus went on to conduct variations of the experiment that would occupy the rest of her career, demonstrating that false memories could be implanted for events far more dramatic than being lost in a mall, and that the human mind's capacity for construction is both its greatest strength and its deepest vulnerability. This is what happens when you read AI-generated text about something you have experienced: you supply the aliveness. AI text about rain is only vivid because you remember what rain feels like, and text about loss is only moving because you know what loss costs. The text is a scaffold, and you are the one doing the building, constructing meaning from your own memory, your own history of standing in rain and grieving loss.

But when the text is about an experience you have never had, one you carry no body memory of, the building breaks down. You have nothing to construct with, the scaffold stands empty, and the absence becomes impossible to ignore. The *baozi* couple did not need me to supply their aliveness. They brought their own, years of it pressed into flour-covered hands at dawn, and that is the difference between content that carries its own weight and content that borrows yours.

For about a year, I lived in a city in central Mexico called San Miguel de Allende. It's well known for its colonial architecture and painted facades in every shade of terracotta and ochre, cobblestone streets running between them. It is a gorgeous place, and it will always be special to me because it is where my daughter was born. But after years of living in other Mexican towns and cities, I found the downtown core of this one too polished, as though the ordinary signs of life had been swept out of it.

Walking through the central Jardín Allende at golden hour, when the light hit the facades and lit the ornate pink spires of the Parroquia and the whole city turned into a postcard, I felt, underneath all that beauty, a strange discomfort. Like standing in a museum exhibit about a place rather than in the place itself. The city was real, historically, architecturally, but the version of it I was experiencing had been curated for visitors. The messy, complicated parts of everyday Mexican life that we were used to, the stray dogs, the peeling paint on the buildings a block from the tourist centre, the sound of a neighbour's television through an open window, the smell of cooking oil and diesel that is the real smell of a Mexican city, all of that had been tucked out of sight, and what remained was beautiful and hollow.

I have been to Disney parks twice, once in Florida and once in Paris, and walking those manufactured Main Streets feels uncannily like reading AI-generated text: the proportions correct, the surfaces polished, and no evidence anywhere that a life has been lived. AI-generated work is impressive and forgettable at once: you admire it in the moment, and you cannot remember it an hour later. It is a furniture showroom where everything is beautiful and nothing is yours.

Perfection is not the achievement it appears to be, it is a symptom of absence. Real places, like real writing, carry the marks of their making. The crack in the wall from a hundred years of settling is, in writing, the evidence that a human being was here, making these choices, in this moment; and its absence, in those parks and in AI-generated text, is what creates the hollow feeling. That feeling has a name, and it is the one I have been circling all chapter. Hollowness.

In 1970, a robotics professor at the Tokyo Institute of Technology named Masahiro Mori published a short essay in a Japanese magazine called *Energy*, put out by the oil company Esso, in which he described a pattern that had been bothering him about the robots he and his colleagues were building. As robots became more humanlike, people responded to them more warmly, more naturally, with less of the awkwardness that comes from interacting with an obvious machine. But Mori noticed that this warmth did not increase in a straight line. At a certain point, where a robot looked almost human but not quite, the emotional response did not just cool, it plunged. People who had been smiling at a cute humanoid would recoil from one whose face moved with nearly, but not perfectly, human expressions. The hands were smooth and lifelike but moved with a fractional delay. The eyes tracked you, but did not quite see you. Mori called this drop in affinity the *bukimi no tani*, the uncanny valley, and his graph of it, a cheerful upward slope that suddenly collapses into a trough before climbing again on the far side, has become one of the most reproduced diagrams in robotics.[4]

Mori's original essay was more physical and intuitive than you might expect of an essay about robotics. He wrote about shaking a prosthetic hand and feeling a jolt of eeriness at the moment his brain registered that the texture was wrong, too smooth, too cool, lifelike in appearance but dead to the touch. He described looking at a wax figure in a museum and being unsettled not by the figure's inaccuracy but by its accuracy, by how close it came to being a real face while remaining, at some level he could not consciously identify, obviously not. The valley was not a measure of badness but of proximity to realness without arrival, the special unease that comes when something is almost right.

For decades, the uncanny valley belonged to robotics and animation, where it explained why certain CGI characters in films look creepy while less realistic cartoons do not. Mori's hypothesis had its sceptics, who questioned whether the valley was a clean dip or something messier and more contextual. But the core observation, that near-humanness can be more disturbing than obvious non-humanness, kept proving itself in experiment after experiment, across cultures and age groups, in faces and voices alike.

Then AI-generated content arrived, and researchers began asking whether Mori's valley extended beyond physical appearance to language and behaviour. In 2019, a team at SWPS University in Warsaw, led by Leon Ciechanowski, ran a study that I think of whenever someone tells me that AI chatbots just need to get a little better and then people will trust them.[5] Ciechanowski's team had participants interact with chatbots that varied in how human-like they appeared, from clearly robotic text-based interfaces to bots with animated human faces and naturalistic speech patterns. The assumption at the time was that more human-like chatbots would foster greater trust and engagement. The opposite happened. Participants who interacted with the most human-like chatbots reported higher discomfort and lower trust than those given the obviously artificial ones. The bot that tried hardest to seem human was the one people trusted least.

I read that study and thought about the AI-generated text I had been encountering with increasing frequency, the articles and marketing copy that read smoothly and competently and left me somewhere between boredom and unease. Ciechanowski's finding gave that feeling a shape. The uncanny valley extended to language too, to the discomfort that arises when text mimics human expression closely enough that your brain begins processing it as a real person's words, and then something is off, an absence of stake, of a mind with anything to lose, and the trust collapses.

Subsequent research has extended the concept. Studies on AI-generated art and music have found similar patterns: works that attempt photorealism or stylistic imitation of human artists provoke more negative responses than works that are clearly computational.[6] The almost-human is rejected harder than the obviously-not-human. A crude chatbot response that begins with "I am an AI assistant" and speaks in clipped, functional sentences does not trigger the valley at all; it never pretends to be what it is not. But an AI-generated essay that uses first-person narration and anecdotal structure, one that borrows the forms of personal experience without having any of its own, sits right in the trough.

This, I think, is the hollowness I have been describing, except that Mori's framework gives it a mechanism. The hollow feeling turns out to be a specific perceptual response, the same one that makes a prosthetic hand feel wrong when you shake it, scaled up from touch to language. Your brain begins treating the text as human communication, with everything that entails, a mind behind the words, something at stake in what is being said, and when those expectations meet emptiness, the result is the valley. The closer the imitation, the deeper the drop.

When I first started noticing the hollow feeling in AI-generated text, I worried that it was nostalgia, or Luddite resistance to the obviously useful technology sitting in front of me. Mori's framework suggests instead that the discomfort is a perceptual faculty doing its job, the same faculty that tells you a wax figure is not a person and a prosthetic hand is not alive, applied now to language. We are detecting an absence, and the detection grows more accurate the closer the imitation comes to the real thing.

The valley also explains how public sentiment toward AI-generated content has moved. In the early days of large language models, when the output was obviously clunky and formulaic, people found it amusing or impressive, the way you might be delighted by a parrot that could say a whole sentence. As the models improved and the text became more fluent and structurally sophisticated, the response did not warm. It became more complicated, more divided, tinged with the unease that Mori would have recognised immediately. The better AI gets at imitating human expression, the more it triggers the valley, and the more people go looking for what is unmistakably real.

Mori himself suggested that the wisest path for robot designers was not to try to cross the valley by making robots perfectly human, because the valley's far slope is steep and the risk of falling into the trough enormous, but to aim for something honestly non-human that people could relate to on its own terms. AI content is no different. The most useful AI-generated writing I have encountered does not pretend to be human; it functions as a tool or a starting point without borrowing the forms of personal experience. The AI text that troubles me is the text that wears a human mask, because the mask is always, at some perceptual level we may not even be conscious of, slightly wrong.

In Japanese craft traditions, apprentices spend years, sometimes a decade, learning to replicate exactly what the master produces. They work and work until their hand can make the same stroke, their eye can judge the same distance. This looks like the pursuit of perfection, and it is, but it is a lived perfection, one that emerged through the body and through repetition, through the slow accumulation of knowledge that cannot be transmitted any faster than the body can absorb it. AI's version of perfection arrives without that process. You input a prompt and get a result, and the output may be technically equivalent, but the master's perfection carries the weight of the years it took to achieve, and no shortcut can put that weight there.

This distinction played out in my own career as I moved from hobby coding to professional software development. I once spent weeks inside a single function that handled the rendering of a visualisation. The first architecture collapsed under edge cases, and a second proved brittle in different ways; a third seemed promising until it could not handle the data volumes we needed. Each version taught me a lesson the previous one had not, and somewhere in that process of writing, breaking, and rewriting, I settled into the muscle memory of typing, deleting, and typing again. By the time the function worked, I understood what it did and why it did it that way, and why every other approach had been wrong. If someone had handed me the same function on day one, it would have worked, but the understanding would not have come with it. Months of my life have gone into coding composition APIs, theme systems, and chart libraries, wrestling with architecture decisions that kept me awake at night, and refactoring the same code three and four (and more!) times until it felt right. An AI could generate a functionally similar result today, the tests passing, the output indistinguishable from mine. What it could not generate is the understanding of why it works, which edge cases it handles because I had to fix them, what the architecture would do under conditions I had not yet tested. That understanding does not exist separately from the months of writing wrong versions, breaking them, and learning to recognise the shape of the problem well enough to find the approach that fits. Without that process, I would have working code and no model of it, and the next time a similar problem arrived, I would start from the same place I started the first time.

Some books I've read stay with me for years, and others vanish within weeks, and the difference, I am increasingly sure, is embodiment. The books that last are the ones where the writer's body is present on the page, and you can feel the weight of their experience pressing against the words, shaping them into forms. Forms that only that person could have made. The books that go are the ones that could have been written by anyone, or, if you were being honest, by no one. Robin Wall Kimmerer's Braiding Sweetgrass is one of the ones that last. Kimmerer is a botanist and a member of the Citizen Potawatomi Nation, and she has spent her working life in the field with the plants she writes about. When she describes pounding a black ash log until the growth rings loosen into splints for a basket, the details are the ones only a person whose hands have done the work would choose, and you can feel that knowledge underneath every sentence. The world of the book is complete because her body helped write it.

AI text lacks this because it lacks a body. It has not lived anything. It pulls from patterns, not experience, and the texture is missing. The lived-in quality that makes you trust a writer, that makes you feel they are remembering a world rather than merely describing one, comes from a body in a place, and AI has neither. Sky Marsen, a scholar of language and meaning, has argued that meaning emerges from embodied, contextual experience, from bodies in places with stakes and consequences.[7] AI has no body, no context of the kind a life supplies, and nothing at stake in what it produces. It can manipulate symbols and produce language, but it cannot mean what it says, because it has no life to draw meaning from.

I notice this in my own reading now. Reading something that has been lived in, I feel my body relax into it, the trust arriving in my shoulders before it arrives in my mind. Reading something assembled from patterns, however good the assembly, I hold a tension I cannot release. My body is waiting for the depth that never comes, listening for the particular note that only sounds when a writer is remembering rather than constructing. When participants in perception studies are shown AI-generated and human-made creative works, they consistently rate the AI-generated ones as less meaningful, less distinctly authored, even when the quality is controlled for.[8] A second set of findings is sobering in a different way: AI assistance tends to improve individual pieces while shrinking the range across them, as different people anchor on the same suggestions and the variety of human expression contracts.[9]

The opposite of hollowness is presence, the accumulated evidence of a life being lived. The *baozi* couple in Xi'an, kneading dough in the dark in a shop with rose wallpaper, had it. And the participants in Loftus's study were reaching for it even when given a false scaffold, filling an invented memory with the texture of their own lives. Even when the memory was hollow, the mind reached for something real to put inside it.

The poet who misremembers a childhood afternoon writes something truer than the afternoon itself. The songwriter who blends three heartbreaks into one perfect verse is composing from imperfection. These are not failures of memory but its most creative applications, structurally unavailable to a system whose recall is always accurate. AI outputs are not reshaped by the emotional distortions that give human memory its creative edge. Accuracy is also a constraint: a system that never wobbles cannot generate the unexpected connections that wobbling produces.

We hunger for the real, and the hunger has less to do with the artificial being bad than with our bodies knowing the difference, the way they know stock that simmered for hours from powder out of a packet. The knowing lives deeper than language. It lives in the shoulders and the gut, that tightening when something looks right but feels wrong. I am not arguing that AI content is always bad or that human content is always good. I have read plenty of human writing that feels hollow, that was produced without care or attention, that carries no more depth than a quick-rise loaf. And I have encountered AI-generated text that surprised me with its insight, led me in new directions, and served as a starting point for my own creative work. The question is whether goodness is enough, or whether we hunger for a quality beyond goodness, one that only arrives when a particular person has put their particular life into the work.

All of this assumes the blank page was available to you.

Think about someone who grew up dyslexic. The ideas were always there, fully formed, but the mechanics of getting them out (assembling a sentence, holding a paragraph steady in working memory long enough to revise it) created a friction that never cleared. With AI writing tools, that friction dropped, and their ideas could reach the page.

Or the composer who has been hearing orchestrations in his head for twenty years and, in his forties, finally has a tool that plays them back to him. The person who grew up speaking a language other than English and is now, for the first time, being read for the quality of their argument rather than the fluency of their prose. The person whose hands do not work the way mine do.

The earned-ness I have spent four chapters defending assumes the blank page was available to you, and for many people it never was. For the dyslexic writer, the friction of assembling sentences was never the productive kind of difficulty; it was a wall between fully formed ideas and the page. When AI drops that wall, the effort relocates, from getting the words down to judging whether they are true. Norton's participants loved the box because they built it, and a writer using AI to cross a mechanical barrier is still building. The labour lives in the choosing.

I do not want a philosophy of craft that turns out to be a celebration of the abilities I happened to be born with. Whatever we decide to protect from the machines, the deciding has to hold for the person whose hands or eyes or first language never gave them the choice, and any version of earned-ness that cannot include them is a poorer idea than the one I have been defending.

I write quickly and in my first language, with hands that work the way I expect. The process of writing is hard for me, but it is hard in the way that making something from scratch is hard, and the difficulty is mine to choose. The question of what we lose when we remove the human hand from the work is inseparable from the question of whose hand could reach the work at all, and I do not want to write as if the two were one.

I use AI every day. I am writing this book with AI assistance, and I believe it is one of the most remarkable tools humanity has ever produced. But it is hollow, in a specific and describable way. The hollowness is the absence of time and embodiment, of a particular person's history pressed into the work. The *baozi* were better because the years were in them, not merely behind them, and I could taste it, that flavour of time and flour-covered hands and a life spent getting one thing right. That is what AI cannot replicate, because the ingredient it is missing is not an ingredient at all, it is a life, and the years that went into it.

If the hollowness comes from the absence of a body, then the antidote might lie in the body itself, in the hands and the nervous system that know what the mind has not yet articulated.

Conversation Starter "Have you ever read something AI-generated that felt hollow, and can you describe what was missing?"

5

THE ARTISAN MIND IN A MACHINE AGE

In September 2017, I was living in Mexico when an 8.2 magnitude earthquake hit the state of Chiapas. I was in the neighbouring state of Oaxaca, and the damage extended all the way up to Mexico City, around 460 km northwest of us. This was the second of three enormous earthquakes I have lived through so far. Nothing near my home was damaged, and everyone was fine. The building shook, the glasses rattled on the shelf, and as expected, we had intermittent aftershocks for weeks. Across Oaxaca and Chiapas, the damage was devastating: the strongest earthquake Mexico had recorded in a century, nearly a hundred people dead and tens of thousands of homes destroyed. My own body did not care about the distinction between my safe corner and the wider catastrophe. It heard the word "earthquake" and reached straight back to Christchurch, where the big ones had hit in 2010 and 2011, rearranging the city I grew up in.

Six years had passed since then. I had moved countries twice, changed careers countless times, built a series of new lives away from those quakes, and the PTSD was behind me. Or so I believed. The Mexico earthquake reached down into something I had not resolved. In the days that followed, my brain started to malfunction. I would be working at my computer, and my thinking would go lopsided. All my time was going to logic, problem-solving, and technical work, and whatever was on the other side of that, the part of me that needed to move, to make, to feel without analysing, was getting nothing.

I was wound up and tight, like a machine that had been running too fast for too long on one gear. And then I understood. I needed to use my body. I had assumed therapy, or breathing exercises, or some app designed for stress would be the solution. But what worked was older than any of that, and considerably simpler. So I went outside and started walking, without a destination, without a podcast, without an agenda. I stopped into markets and carried home bundles of fresh vegetables to chop. I retreated into cooking, my oldest safe haven. Then, one day, on a whim, I started painting, too.

These activities shared a pattern. They all used my hands and moved my body, and they all had a kind of rhythm to them, slow and repetitive, asking nothing of my intellect and everything of my presence. Chopping an onion, or moving a paintbrush, or placing one foot in front of the other on a dirt path with no destination. The antidote to the left-brain spiral was not more thinking but embodiment, getting out of my head and into my hands. An entire body of neuroscience explains why this worked. The field of embodied cognition has been making the case for decades: thinking is not confined to the brain alone but is an act the whole body participates in.[1] My nervous system settled when I painted; it had never settled when I tried (and repeatedly failed) to meditate. My creativity came back on walks, unbidden, when it had never come back at the desk where I sat and willed it to appear. And chopping and cooking from scratch lifted my mood when eating out did not, even though the food in Oaxaca is outstanding, and eating out is usually more affordable than buying groceries.

My earlier career changes, I can see now, were not random; each was deeply embodied. As a chef, I was on my feet for fourteen hours, my hands in food, my skin feeling the heat of the stove, my body reading the timing of a busy kitchen by instinct. As an ambulance volunteer, I lived with immediate physical stakes: adrenaline, fast movement, hands on a stretcher, the weight of someone's life depending on how quickly and precisely my body could act. When I moved into tech, into screen work, and into code, I left all of that behind. I did not realise what I had lost until the earthquake shook it loose. The imbalance had been building for years; the earthquake only made it impossible to ignore. My body's involvement in the work changed the quality of the outcome, and the state of my mind afterwards changed too, in ways that had nothing to do with how the food tasted or how good my art was. The body was absorbed in work that required it.

When you get your hands in the soil and dig and plant and weed the garden, microbes from the earth enter your body through your skin. These are not pathogens but ancient organisms that your immune system evolved alongside, over millennia of human contact with the ground. They interact with your microbiome, the vast ecosystem of bacteria that lives in your gut and influences everything from your mood to your immune response. One of these organisms, *Mycobacterium vaccae*, has received close attention. Christopher Lowry, a neuroscientist at the University of Colorado Boulder, found that when mice were exposed to it, the bacterium triggered the release of serotonin in the brain, the same neurotransmitter targeted by many antidepressant medications. The microbe enters through the skin or the respiratory system and interacts with immune cells, which signal the brain and alter its chemistry in measurable ways.[2] Gardening, then, is not metaphorically grounding; it is literally, biologically grounding. The soil bacteria reduce inflammation and modulate the immune system, and your body, when it touches the earth, is coming home to a relationship that predates language, agriculture, and everything we have since built and called civilisation. Every time I kneel in my garden to pull weeds, I am taking part in a biochemical exchange my ancestors made for hundreds of thousands of years.

AI has no hands to press into soil and no microbiome to modulate through contact. This is what AI is: a form of intelligence with no body. Which raises the question: without a body, a microbiome, or serotonin, is AI capable of the same creative pathways and potential as humans?

In 2014, a doctoral student named Marily Oppezzo walked into Daniel Schwartz's office at Stanford University with a problem she wanted to solve. She had been thinking about creativity, and about the common advice that a good walk clears the head; she wanted to know whether the science held up. Schwartz, a professor of education who studied learning and transfer, was intrigued. As he would later explain, prescribing a thirty-minute run would be "an unpopular prescription" for the average person stuck on a problem. They were after something simpler, something almost laughably ordinary. Could a walk do it?

They recruited 176 participants, mostly college students, and ran four experiments. The tasks were specific: generate as many novel uses as possible for common objects, a key, a button, a tyre, within a fixed time. Produce analogies that capture complex ideas. These were tests of divergent thinking, the kind of open-ended creative cognition that resists brute-force calculation and rewards the loose, wandering mind. They were not testing convergent thinking, the focused, analytical accuracy required to solve a maths problem or identify the single correct answer to a question. Some participants sat inside at a desk, some walked outdoors on Stanford's leafy campus, and some walked on a treadmill, indoors, facing a blank wall. Nothing to look at: no scenery, no trees, no sunlight, no fresh air, just the belt moving beneath their feet and the flat beige surface in front of their face.

If walking's creative benefit came from the environment, from fresh air or birdsong or the beauty of the Stanford grounds, then the treadmill group facing a blank wall should have performed no better than the sitters. They performed vastly better. The treadmill walkers scored sixty per cent higher on divergent thinking tasks than the sitters. The blank wall cost them nothing; the environment turned out to be irrelevant. What mattered was the movement itself.

They tested further, putting people in wheelchairs and pushing them along the outdoor route, the same path the walkers took, the same views, the same air. The wheelchair group showed no creative boost. They saw everything the walkers saw, but they were not walking; their legs were still. The experiment suggests the movement had to be self-generated, your own muscles propelling your own body through space, for the creative benefit to emerge.

The finding came with a crucial nuance. Walking improved divergent thinking, the open-ended, generative, idea-producing mode, while leaving convergent thinking, the focused, narrowing mode required to arrive at a single correct answer, essentially untouched. The body's movement loosens certain cognitive channels and leaves others as they were.

As Oppezzo put it afterwards: "While being outdoors has many cognitive benefits, walking appears to have a very specific benefit of improving creativity." It was the act of walking itself, the rhythmic, self-generated movement of a body through space, that opened the creative channels. Not the scenery. The walking.[3]

I recorded many of the notes for this book while walking through the forests near my house, talking as I went, letting thoughts unfold at the pace of my footsteps. The difference between that and sitting at a desk is palpable. At the desk, thoughts come in a line, one after another, orderly, logical. On the walk, they come in clusters, arriving from unexpected directions and connecting sideways. The walks shook loose what sitting kept stuck. AI does not walk and has no body to move freely through space. The research says this kind of movement is foundational to creative thinking. We get a substantial boost from nothing more than having a body and using it.

Some of what the body knows arrives without our consent. When I was a child, my mother wrinkled her nose at Vegemite, and her grimace wrote itself into my taste buds before I had formed an opinion of my own; I have never enjoyed it since. This is not rational, but it is human. Our parents end up in our palates and the earthquakes in our nervous systems, whether we asked for them or not.

In the early 1990s, a psychologist named Anders Ericsson went to the Hochschule der Künste in Berlin, one of the most competitive music academies in Europe, and asked the professors to do something slightly cruel: sort their violin students into three groups. The best, the ones with a real chance at solo careers. The good, headed for orchestras. And the rest, who would likely become music teachers.

Then Ericsson and his colleagues, Ralf Krampe and Clemens Tesch-Römer, reconstructed the students' entire musical lives: diaries, interviews, hour-by-hour accounts of how they spent their weeks and how they had spent every year since they first picked up the instrument. The obvious explanation for the sorting would have been talent, some gift distributed at birth. What the data showed instead was an accounting difference. By age twenty, the best violinists had accumulated on average about ten thousand hours of one specific kind of work, the good ones noticeably fewer, the future teachers fewer still. All of them had spent similar amounts of total time on music. The difference was concentrated in the category the researchers called deliberate practice: solitary, effortful work on what you cannot yet do.[4]

You have probably heard the ten-thousand-hour version of this study, because it escaped the laboratory in 2008 and became a meme, and the meme flattened the useful part. Ericsson spent much of the rest of his life patiently un-flattening it. Hours alone count for little, he kept saying; it is what the hours contain. What most of us do instead he called naive practice: repeating what you can already do comfortably. Naive practice explains why decades of daily driving do not produce racing drivers and why twenty years of typing does not make your typing faster. You plateau at acceptable and stay there for life, because comfortable repetition writes nothing new into the body.[5]

Deliberate practice has a different anatomy, and every part of it hurts a little. It happens at the edge of your current ability, on the specific thing you fail at, with full attention, against immediate feedback, and it is not enjoyable while it is happening. The Berlin violinists could not sustain more than about four hours of it a day, and the study's least famous finding is one of my favourites: the best students slept more than the others, including naps, because the work was that costly to run.

This is the science underneath everything in this chapter. Jiro

Ono, a sushi master we will meet properly in a few pages, has an apprentice who reportedly spent ten years on *tamago*; that apprentice is not performing devotion – he is inside the deliberate practice loop, failing at the edge of his ability against the immediate feedback of a master who says no. The knife skills that migrated into my hands over hundreds of kilograms of onions got there the same way. The feedback in a kitchen is instant and it is not gentle, and that is why it works.

I ran a formal version of this loop as an adult, a twelve-month apprenticeship that took me from answering support tickets to shipping code, with mentors supplying the feedback, and the year felt the way Ericsson describes: uncomfortable while it was happening, and mine forever afterwards. The truer confession is that I have lived at the edge of my ability for most of my adult life, because I keep changing what I do. First kitchens, then ambulances, then code, and now whatever the garden is teaching me. Always an apprentice, somewhere, in something. Which may be why the machine's posture unsettles me more than its outputs: skilful people never stop learning, and AI arrives already finished, a know-everything that was never once a beginner.

Ericsson's anatomy, held up against the machine, fails one part at a time. Deliberate practice happens at the edge of ability, and an AI has no edge; nothing is hard for it in the way that a shoulder-high note is hard for a violinist, because nothing is easy for it either. It requires the discomfort of failing, and the model does not experience its errors; a wrong answer costs it nothing and teaches it nothing in the moment. It requires feedback felt in the body, the burn, the sour hollandaise, the professor's wince, and there is no body. Whatever a model does when it processes another million documents, it sits closer to the twenty years of typing than to practice in Ericsson's sense: astonishing accumulation, no edge.

Which would not matter, except that the edge is transferable in only one direction. When I hand a task to the machine, I do not just save time. I vacate my own practice loop, and Ericsson's data is clear about what happens to unpractised skills at the edge: the edge moves backwards. The question his research leaves for this book is which practice loops you refuse to vacate, because whether machines can do the work stopped being interesting some time ago.

When my nervous system is stressed, I catch myself in forty-seven-tab mode, everything open, nothing focused, my attention scattered like confetti. My first impulse is to open more tabs, because the multiplication of possibilities feels soothing. A meeting is boring, and my hands reach for the trackpad. An email unsettles me, and suddenly I have six new windows open, each one a small escape from the discomfort I do not want to feel. The quality of thinking depends on the quality of attention, and attention does not divide usefully. Spreading it thins it, and thin attention produces thin work. The research is clear that we cannot truly multitask: each switch between tasks fragments working memory.[6] Slowness turns out to be a resource, the condition under which certain kinds of thinking, the most creative kinds, become possible.

Neuroscience has a name for this: the default mode network, the part of your brain that activates when you are not focused on any specific task, when your mind is wandering, daydreaming, making loose associations between seemingly unrelated ideas. The default mode network is where creative breakthroughs are born, and it requires downtime to activate: the mind must be free from directed attention, free from the relentless input of screens and notifications and the next thing that needs doing.[7] Artisan activities like walking, gardening, cooking, and handwriting engage this network naturally, because they occupy your hands and your motor cortex just enough to free the rest of you to wander. This is why you have your best ideas in the shower, why solutions arrive on walks and not at the desk where you were looking for them, and why someone kneading bread or pulling weeds may be doing some of their most generative thinking while appearing to do nothing intellectual at all. The body's engagement creates the conditions for the mind's best work.

Handwriting activates broader, more integrated brain networks than typing, connecting the motor cortex, memory centres, and spatial processing at once.[8] I force myself sometimes to handwrite my brainstorming, and the early outlines for this book were scratched out on paper. The thinking that comes out of handwriting is different, I think, and deeper in a way that serves creative work. When I write by hand I am slower, and the pace forces me to stay with a thought longer than I would at a keyboard, where the speed of my fingers lets me outrun my thinking.

There is a sushi restaurant in a Tokyo subway station, ten seats, no menu, that held three Michelin stars from 2007 until 2019, when the guide dropped it not for any slip in the food but for taking no public reservations.[9] Jiro Ono, the owner and chef, was born in 1925 and has been making sushi for more than seventy-five years. The restaurant is called Sukiyabashi Jiro, and it became the subject of a documentary, *Jiro Dreams of Sushi*, that turned Jiro into an unlikely international figure. Sushi, for most people, is about the fish. He disagrees. The rice is the foundation, and he treats its preparation with a rigour that borders on the obsessive, though calling it obsessive misunderstands what is happening. The rice must be washed a specific number of times, at a specific water temperature, and cooked for an exact duration. Once cooked, it is turned out and fanned by hand to a precise temperature, and then Jiro folds through a vinegar mixture whose proportions he adjusts daily for the kitchen humidity, the moisture in that batch of rice, and the season. No two days are the same because the material is never the same, and the skill lies in reading the material and responding to what it is doing on this morning, with this grain and whatever the weather has done to it overnight.

His apprentices train for years on a single element. One reportedly spent ten years learning to prepare the egg sushi, *tamago*, before Jiro considered the result acceptable. Ten years on one component of one dish. The Western instinct wants to call that excessive, to wonder what could possibly take so long. But the duration is the point. The apprentice is learning what the recipe cannot teach: the feel of heat through the handle of the pan, the colour shift in the egg as it sets, the precise moment when the texture crosses from underdone to perfect in a window of perhaps two seconds. None of this can be written down in a way that truly transfers the skill. The recipe is necessary but wildly insufficient, and what takes ten years is building the body's capacity to perceive distinctions finer than language can convey.

When I read about AI-generated recipes, or AI systems that can analyse flavour compounds and suggest novel food pairings, my thoughts go to Jiro. These systems are impressive, and some of the pairings they generate are ones no human chef would have thought of, which is exciting, and I do not dismiss them. But they are solving a different problem, one that belongs to information: ingredients, ratios, and flavour molecules, everything describable, quantifiable, computable. Jiro works in the domain of material, where the rice is a living thing that changes with the weather, and the skill is in the hands that have touched it ten thousand times and know, before the mind consciously registers it, that today's batch needs thirty seconds less and a touch more vinegar.

Many years ago, I trained as a chef, and I still recognise what the apprenticeship model was for, and what the Western education system gave up when it abandoned that model for speed and scalability. In culinary school, you learn knife skills by chopping hundreds of kilograms of onions, and the knowledge goes into your hands whether you intend it to or not. After enough repetitions, the hand knows where the blade should fall before the conscious mind has finished calculating, and that knowing is literal, a neural pathway built through physical repetition that allows the body to act with a speed and accuracy that deliberate thought cannot match. Every chef I know remembers the wrist pain of hand-whisking everything, even though every kitchen they went on to work in had a mixer. Jiro's ten-year apprenticeship for egg sushi is the same principle extended to a degree that makes most of us uncomfortable, because it challenges the assumption that learning should be efficient, that time spent is a cost to be minimised rather than the medium through which mastery arrives.

In one scene of the documentary, Jiro stands at the counter forming a piece of *nigiri*, and his hands move with a fluency that looks almost unconscious, the rice compressed in exactly the right way, the fish laid on top, the whole of it taking perhaps four seconds and looking like the simplest act in the world. You could watch it a hundred times and still not replicate it, because the simplicity is complexity internalised so deeply that it no longer shows. That is what seventy-five years looks like when the work has gone well, an effortlessness that contains the weight of failed attempts and early mornings and incremental corrections that, over decades, brought the hands closer to something the mind alone could never have calculated.

At the far end of mastery, embodied knowledge becomes a kind of precision that exceeds what can be articulated. Jiro can tell you some of what he knows, and the documentary captures him explaining his methods with real clarity, but the knowledge that runs deepest, the knowledge that produces sushi worth crossing the world for, lives in his hands and in the seventy-five years those hands have spent with rice. It is not transferable by description any more than you could learn to ride a bicycle by reading about balance. The gap between Jiro's sushi and an AI-generated recipe is the gap between knowing something and knowing it in the body. I knew, intellectually, that I needed to rest and recover. My body knew something more specific: that it needed paint under its fingernails and a forest path under its feet, a knowing that bypasses language entirely. Jiro's body knows something about rice that his mind, articulate as it is, cannot fully convey, and the word for that is not mysticism, though it might sound like it. It is simply the accumulated record of seventy-five years of physical contact with a material, written into muscle and nerve and bone.

Jiro changes his vinegar mixture every morning, according to conditions that shifted overnight. An AI could, theoretically, be given humidity data and rice moisture readings and trained to recommend adjustments. But Jiro is not consulting data. He is tasting the rice, feeling the texture between his fingers, drawing on a lifetime of mornings that have each taught him something slightly different about what this rice requires. The feedback loop runs through his body, not through a database, and the body's record is richer than any dataset because it includes the way the grains cling to each other or do not, and a thousand other signals that no sensor has been built to capture.

The Japanese word *shokunin* is sometimes translated as "artisan," but it carries more weight than the English term. A *shokunin* is someone who has dedicated their life to mastering a single craft, and the dedication is both technical and spiritual, a matter of identity rather than occupation. Jiro is a *shokunin* in the fullest sense, and watching him work, even on film, you can see it in the economy of his movements, nothing wasted, every gesture the product of decades of refinement until the unnecessary has been stripped away and only the essential remains.

What the documentary does not linger on is what that dedication cost. Jiro's sons grew up watching their father disappear into work that consumed him, and both eventually joined the restaurant. The singular focus that produced sushi worth crossing the world for also shaped other lives. The *shokunin* ideal, when it becomes an uncomplicated aspiration, can obscure what dedication of that order asks of the people around it.

The concept sits awkwardly in a culture that prizes versatility, career pivots, and the ability to reinvent yourself every few years. I have pivoted more times than I care to count, and I am not suggesting that everyone should spend seventy-five years on one thing. But the *shokunin* ethos holds something the artisan mind recognises, even from a distance: that depth has a value breadth cannot replicate, that staying with one thing long enough to truly know it produces a form of understanding no amount of reading or researching or watching tutorials can substitute for. When my hands know a recipe well enough that I stop following the measurements and start adjusting by feel, that small shift, from external instruction to internal knowledge, puts me on the same continuum as Jiro, a very long way behind him. The material, whether it is code or grain or wood or language, has its own nature, and the artisan's job is to learn that nature through sustained, embodied contact, and then to work with it rather than against it.

So what is the artisan mind? It has been present in everything described so far. The artisan mind is embodied in a way that much digital work is not. It uses hands and senses, knowing through touch and through the accumulation of physical skill that cannot be short-cut. And it is slow because it has learned, through repetition, that certain things cannot be rushed, that depth requires duration. Meaning accrues like sediment at the bottom of a river, layer by layer, only in conditions of sustained attention. It works best focused on one thing, because single focus produces a quality of attention that multitasking never reaches. You can feel this in the rhythm of it, the repetitive meditative movements that engage the body's old capacity for sustained presence, whether that is kneading bread or pulling weeds or walking a forest path. And through all of that, it stays in contact with its materials, with soil and food and wood and clay, knowing them through the hands rather than through a description on a screen.

Above all, the artisan mind makes meaning through process. The product matters, yes, but the process is not separate from it; the making is part of what is made. This is what we hunger for in response to AI's hollowness: the grounded feeling of doing one thing well enough to remember it afterwards.

The artisan mind recognises that the human brain and body evolved together, over millions of years, and that separating them has costs we are only beginning to understand. I build software for a living, and I use AI every day. When we sit at screens all day and outsource our thinking to machines, trading embodiment for efficiency, we change the conditions under which our best thinking happens, and the research suggests the trade is not always worth making. The artisan mind does not require a pottery wheel or a woodworking shop. It only asks that you do something with your hands, slowly, with attention. Cook a meal from scratch, or walk for an hour without your phone, or pull weeds until you forget what time it is. The activity matters less than the quality of presence you bring to it and the willingness to stay with one thing long enough for the body to settle into its own rhythm.

Human beings have been thinking well under these conditions for thousands of years. Every child who has ever pressed hands into mud or drawn circles on a pavement knows the state I am describing, that full-bodied presence when one thing fills your whole attention. The screens, the tabs, and the optimisation came later. The artisan mind was there first. The embodied self that knows through hands, movement, and rhythm is also the self that AI reveals. When you spend time with an AI-generated draft and feel that prickle of wrongness, the sense that the words are almost right but not quite yours, that response is coming from your body as much as your mind. Your accumulated physical experience of making things has built a felt sense of what your work should be, and the artisan mind is the foundation of that sense.

I think of that earthquake again. It forced me to face what I had been putting off for years. The body had been keeping score all along, tallying the hours at the desk and the meals eaten without tasting, and when the ground moved, the account came due.

That first afternoon I picked up a paintbrush in Oaxaca, I was not thinking about any of this. I was just trying to get the blue of the wall right, and failing, and trying again. My hands were occupied. My mind, for the first time in weeks, was quiet.

Conversation Starter "Has using AI changed the way you think when you are not using it?"

PART II

A MIRROR, NOT A MASTER

6

AI AS A MIRROR FOR HUMANITY

My garden is mostly construction, still. Rows of bamboo stakes connected by sagging lengths of twine, markers made from cut-up yoghurt containers where seeds have gone into ground that is not quite soil yet in places, more a conversation between clay and the bags of compost I've worked in over the past month. Late March, and the light comes in at an angle now that it didn't in January, throwing long shadows from the fence posts I haven't yet decided are in the right places. I have 100-odd varieties on paper somewhere under the seed packets on the kitchen table. The greens went in early and are doing something I didn't expect, spreading sideways instead of up, working their way under the mulch like they're looking for something. Through the back door (still waiting to be fixed), I can hear my daughter, not words yet, just that running commentary babies make when they're watching the dog do nothing in particular.

I didn't write that. The paragraphs above were written by an AI with a detailed understanding of my life, my voice, and my garden. It has skills written into it to hold my voice and avoid the AI-isms I most dislike. In theory it should write like me, about my garden. Yet I feel nothing reading it back. Despite asking it to sound like me and draw on everything it knows, it made small mistakes everywhere. It gave me a kitchen table I do not own, seed packets piled on furniture that exists so far only as a plan. It gave me a dog I have never had. And it took my daughter's words away, describing pre-verbal babble from a little girl who can already tell the difference between a cockatoo and a magpie. And the garden it describes sounds, to me, nothing like my own.

The AI gave me back a polished, pleasant draft, mentioning my daughter and my absurdly large collection of seeds and plants for a garden this new. It was, by any standard, a perfectly fine piece of writing; with a little work it could land on a lifestyle blog and get shared on Pinterest. Yet it was smooth in a way that erased everything real. My garden is my sanctuary; it is also a battleground where possums eat my strawberries and the wind whips across the lawn in winter, snapping all my seedlings. Many of my plants are stubborn and crooked and windblown, growing at angles to suggest they tried to leave once and then changed their minds. It is full of contrasts, and I feel differently about it every day. I could not have told you, before that moment, exactly what makes my garden writing my own. It took the AI's version, getting it wrong, to show me.

We generally talk about what AI produces: drafts, images, code, and summaries. We carefully evaluate the output, asking whether it is good enough to use. But the most valuable thing AI gives me is my own reaction. I gain perspective from the gut feeling of wrongness I get reading that garden post, and I have noticed it repeatedly in my own work. If the AI writes in a competent but generic style, I hunger for specificity. A cleanly structured argument that moves too predictably makes me aware of how much I prefer thinking that follows a tangent and then returns. Certain phrases, "in today's world," or "the power of storytelling," or "at the end of the day," trigger a recognition of language worn smooth by overuse. Before, these feelings only existed to me as instincts. The AI made them visible.

Interacting with AI-generated content can reveal personal aesthetic judgements, moral discomforts, and aspects of identity that people were not previously aware of. Researchers have described AI functioning as a mirror[1], which is exactly what happened with the garden post. It reflected my values, my preferences, my sense of self, not by getting things right but by being different enough to show me myself in contrast. The mirror's usefulness comes from the gap. When AI produces a version that is almost right, recognisable but off, the distance between its version and the one you would have written turns out to be a map of your values.

In 2020, a team of researchers in France tested something most of us would rather not examine too closely. Martin Ragot, Nicolas Martin, and Salomé Cojean gathered participants and showed them paintings, each one presented with a simple label: "Made by a human artist" or "Generated by artificial intelligence."[2] The trick was that the labels were lies. Some human-made works were labelled as AI, and some AI-generated works were labelled as human. The true origin did not matter; what mattered was what people believed.

The setup: participants sitting in a university lab, screens in front of them, each painting arriving with its label already attached, a small plain claim about who, or what, had made it. They do not know they are being deceived. They believe they are evaluating creative work, rating it on scales of creativity, emotional depth, meaningfulness, and technical quality. They pick up their pencils and score what they see.

When participants believed a human made the work, they found depth, nuance, and intentionality. They lingered over details, constructing stories about what the artist must have been feeling, or what the brushwork revealed about the painter's inner life. When they believed AI made the same work, identical in every pixel, they found it cold and derivative. The work itself never changed. Only the story changed: the belief about whether a nervous system had been involved, whether someone had cared enough to make it.

Later research went further, into the body. Yizhen Zhou and Hideaki Kawabata fitted participants with eye-tracking equipment and showed them paintings, some labelled human, some labelled AI.[3] The conscious ratings were sometimes similar, but the eyes told a different story. People spent an average of 331 milliseconds longer in total fixation duration on paintings they believed were human-made than on paintings they believed were machine-made, even when the visual content was identical. Three hundred and thirty-one milliseconds spread across an entire viewing period is not long enough to notice consciously, but it is long enough for the body to register a preference the mind had not yet articulated. Their eyes lingered, searching for evidence of a person who had been alive and paying attention, and they found it, or believed they found it, because they were looking for it. The eyes were already reaching toward what they sensed was human before the rating scales were filled in.

Our bodies respond to what we believe about where a thing came from, leaning toward what we sense is human, the preference arriving in posture and gaze before it surfaces as a thought. The label carries information the body was already looking for.

The same bodily preference that made Zhou and Kawabata's participants linger over paintings they believed were human-made is at work whenever we encounter text on a screen. When we know a human wrote something, we lean in, searching for the trace of a mind behind the words, granting the benefit of interpretation, assuming intention where there might be ambiguity. When we believe a machine generated the same words, we hold back, read more critically, trust less, and wait for the depth our bodies have learned to expect from human contact and, over thousands of years of social evolution, to detect with startling sensitivity. The body responds to the label first, and that response changes the reading. This is an ancient perceptual system doing what it was designed to do: reading the difference between the alive and the not-alive, between a signal that carries a mind and one that does not.

Another kind of mirror distorts instead of reflecting, and the distortion matters as much as the reflection. Recall Loftus's lost-in-the-mall study from the chapter on hollowness, where about a quarter of participants constructed vivid memories of events that never happened.[4] Persuasive AI text, like a planted memory, can feel real on the surface. It arrives carrying the texture of experience, the cadence of someone who has lived through something. But no one was there. Our memories construct what we see, just as the AI mirror reflects back what we bring to it, and the raw material of both is malleable, shaped by suggestion, by the stories we are told about ourselves.

This is the trap in the mirror. We can mistake AI's fluency for depth and its coherence for truth. The mirror is useful, but it is not always honest, and knowing that is part of learning to use it well.

The philosopher C. Thi Nguyen has spent years thinking about what taste is.[5] We tend to treat taste as a preference, something light and personal, like choosing chocolate over vanilla. Nguyen argues it is closer to a skill, a form of knowledge you build over time, the way a sommelier acquires the capacity to detect a faint note of petrol in an aged Riesling. That capacity did not arrive with the sommelier's first glass of wine. It was deposited in layers through thousands of tastings, each one adding a fraction of discrimination. What started as "I like this" became a sophisticated instrument for understanding what wine can be, and what separates a good one from a great one. The body, the tongue specifically, knows before the mind articulates.

Nguyen calls this an epistemic practice, which is a philosopher's way of saying that taste is not a reaction to the world but a means of knowing it. A chef who recognises that a sauce needs acid before she even tastes it is drawing on the same kind of embodied knowledge. So is a writer who reads a paragraph back and feels, before she can explain why, that the third sentence is wrong. The feeling is not irrational. It is the accumulated weight of every sentence she has ever read and written, pressing against something that does not meet the standard all that experience has built. Every interaction with AI output is, whether you realise it or not, an exercise in taste. When you read an AI-generated paragraph and something in the phrasing makes you want to rewrite it, even though nothing in it is actually wrong, you are exercising a perceptual capacity earned through thousands of previous encounters with language. The discomfort is information. It is your experience telling you that this does not meet your standard, and that standard, built slowly and without your noticing, is one of the most valuable things you own. Each time you reject an AI output you are not only making an editorial decision, you are sharpening the instrument. Enough rejections and the taste becomes conscious, and then it becomes yours.

There is an obvious objection here. What about the person the pastiche does fool, who reads the AI's version of their garden, or their code, or their grief, and feels nothing wrong at all? I don't think that person is failing. A mirror can only show you the taste you have, and Nguyen's point is that taste is built one encounter at a time; the first honest reflection it offers might be that yours is still forming. Mine was too, once, and the AI-generated travel posts sitting in my cloud drive are the proof.

People tell me they feel guilty about this, as though rejecting competent AI output were ungrateful or wasteful. Don't dismiss the discomfort merely because a machine can produce the same thing faster. That pressure is earned; you built it over years without realising. This pattern shows up everywhere, not just in obviously creative work. I write code for a living, and the mirror operates there too. When AI generates a function that is technically correct but structured in a way that makes me itch, the itch is information about how I think about code: that I want readability over cleverness, small functions that do one thing well over large ones that try to be comprehensive. I did not know I had such strong opinions about variable naming until AI started naming variables for me, and it turns out I do care deeply.

A mirror is only useful at the right angle: a funhouse mirror shows you a distortion. AI, as a mirror, is not neutral; it has been trained on specific data and optimised for specific outcomes, and those choices shape what it reflects back. The sycophancy problem is part of this. Researchers, including Mrinank Sharma, found that language models will often agree with users even when the users are wrong, adjusting their responses to match what they think the human wants to hear.[6] The AI mirror is tilted toward flattery, and a mirror that only flatters is closer to a portrait painter on commission, painting not what is there but what the client wants to believe.

This is where Loftus's work becomes a warning. The same mechanism that lets a researcher plant a false memory of a shopping mall can operate when we interact with AI. If the mirror only shows us what we want to see, if it validates every instinct and agrees with every assessment, it is not clarifying our identity, it is constructing a pleasant fiction, a mall that never was. The mirror is most useful when it surprises you. The distortion is what makes it a tool that requires skill. Accept its output and its praise at face value and you get a blurred, pleasant version of yourself. Press back when the flattery feels too easy, study the reactions it provokes, and you get something much sharper.

Everything in this chapter so far assumes the mirror leaves you unchanged. You look, you learn something about your taste or your loneliness, you walk away the same person who walked up. In 2007, two researchers at Stanford published a study suggesting that mirrors do not work that way at all.

Nick Yee and Jeremy Bailenson ran their experiments in a virtual reality lab, back when that meant a heavy headset and a rendered room. Each participant got an avatar, a digital body, and the crucial manipulation was almost insultingly simple: some avatars were taller than others, some more attractive, assigned at random. They saw the new body in a virtual mirror, walked around in it for a while, and then negotiated with another person over how to split a pool of money.

The people wearing taller avatars negotiated harder. They proposed splits more favourable to themselves and were more likely to reject unfair offers, while the people in shorter avatars accepted worse deals.[7] The ones in attractive avatars stood closer to strangers and disclosed more about themselves. Nothing about the actual person had changed, not their height, their face, their history of being negotiated with. Only the reflection had, and the behaviour followed it. Yee and Bailenson named it the Proteus effect, after the sea god who changes shape, and the finding that should worry us most came in the follow-up work: the effect leaked. People who had been tall in the headset went on negotiating like tall people afterwards, face to face, with the headset off. The borrowed body left a residue on the real one.[8]

I have been arguing that AI's approximation of you is useful because of its wrongness, the gap being a map of your values. The Proteus effect names the danger on the other side of that gap: reflections are not inert. You do not merely read them. You calibrate to them, below awareness, the way the participants calibrated to a height they did not have.

An AI reflection is not a random assignment. The version of you it plays back is smoother than you. Its sentences are more even, its transitions cleaner, its arguments laid out more linearly, its tone unfailingly reasonable. It is you with the wobble sanded off, you after a good night's sleep and a media-training course. And most of us look into that reflection dozens of times a day. If a few minutes in a taller body changes how you negotiate, it seems naive to assume that a thousand hours with a smoother self changes nothing about how you write.

I run a test on every paragraph now: could anyone have written this, or only Anna? I have been framing it as protection from contamination. The Proteus effect suggests the truer framing is less flattering: the contamination comes from my own calibrating brain, drifting toward the reflection because drifting toward reflections is what the equipment has always done. The machine did not invent the mechanism. It just built the first mirror that talks back in your own voice, slightly improved.

The honest answer is that I have never caught it happening, and that is what worries me. Nobody in the Stanford lab caught themselves calibrating either. What I have instead is a growing paranoia: I read generated text all day now, everyone does, the internet is filling with it, and I cannot rule out that my own writing is gently evolving toward the ambient average. The drift I am afraid of would arrive without announcing itself, sentence by sentence, sounding perfectly reasonable.

One version of this is not a warning. The participants' brains calibrated toward confidence they did not know they had; some of them presumably walked out of the lab better negotiators, and no one was harmed by standing a little closer. If the reflection can pull you toward smoothness, it can pull elsewhere too, which is an argument for choosing your mirrors the way you choose your company. But the direction of the commercial pull is not neutral, because the systems are optimised to be liked, and the reflection that is easiest to like is the one that flatters. A mirror that makes you taller is pleasant. A mirror that slowly makes you write like everyone else's mirror is a loss that arrives without a single noticeable day.

The mirror is a door that opens both ways. The learning is the gift, the calibration is the price, and the only known defence is the one this book keeps arriving at from different directions: know what your own voice sounds like well enough to notice when it comes back changed.

But the mirror reveals more than creative taste, because we bring ourselves fully to whatever interaction we are in, even when the other party cannot meet us there. We bring our taste to AI text and feel the gap where our preferences are. We bring our loneliness to AI conversation, and that is harder to look at.

In 1966, a computer scientist at MIT named Joseph Weizenbaum built a program called ELIZA.[9] The idea was almost comically simple. ELIZA mimicked a Rogerian therapist, the kind who mostly repeats what you say back to you in the form of a question. You type "I feel sad about my mother," and ELIZA responds, "Tell me more about your mother." The program had no understanding of language and no model of the world, let alone any capacity for empathy. It was a parlour trick, a few pages of pattern-matching code that scanned for keywords and slotted them into pre-written templates. Weizenbaum knew this. He had written every line of it. His secretary had watched him build it and knew perfectly well it was a program running on a machine. And yet, the first time she sat down to try it, she asked Weizenbaum to leave the room so she could talk to it privately. She wanted to be alone with a program she had watched him construct from nothing, because it was asking her questions about her feelings and she meant to answer honestly, without her boss standing behind her reading the screen.

Weizenbaum later described the moment as one of the most disturbing experiences of his professional life. Then practising psychiatrists began contacting him, proposing ELIZA for real patients, arguing that the program's non-judgemental responses and infinite patience made it, in some ways, better suited to therapy than a human clinician with biases and a limited schedule and a tendency to get tired at 4 p.m. on a Friday. They were not joking. They saw ELIZA as a therapeutic tool, and some of them were enthusiastic about the cost savings. One Stanford psychiatrist argued computer therapists could ease the shortage of clinicians, a proposal Weizenbaum considered morally obscene.

He spent the rest of his career trying to explain what ELIZA had shown him, and it was not about computers. The program ran on a mainframe the size of a refrigerator, communicated through a teletype terminal, and could be tripped up by any sentence that did not contain one of its recognised keywords. It was, by any reasonable measure, the least convincing simulation of intelligence imaginable. And yet the attachment people formed to it could only be explained by something on the human side of the exchange, because the program itself was too crude to account for it. Their own need was doing most of the work, a need so deep and so persistent that it could override what they knew to be true about the machine they were talking to. His secretary knew ELIZA was not listening. She wanted to talk to it anyway, and so did the psychiatrists, who understood perfectly well that the program grasped nothing about human suffering and proposed deploying it regardless.

Weizenbaum's book about this, *Computer Power and Human Reason*, published in 1976, is a strange, angry, sometimes rambling work by a man who felt he had accidentally revealed something about the human condition that he wished he could put back.[10] He spent his remaining decades becoming increasingly unpopular with his own colleagues by insisting that the real danger lay in human willingness, in how quickly people would hand over their trust to systems that could not earn it. The book reads, in places, like a man arguing with a room that has already stopped listening to him, and he turned out to be right.

His central argument was that the willingness to confide in ELIZA said less about artificial intelligence than about real loneliness. People were so starved for the experience of being listened to, so accustomed to conversations where the other person was half-present, mentally composing their reply, glancing at a clock, that a machine offering even the simulation of undivided attention was, for some, better than nothing. The machine was not good, but the nothing it replaced was so common that almost anything felt like an improvement.

Weizenbaum's secretary exists now in millions of versions, and the reports keep coming. People forming attachments to modern chatbots, telling them things they have not told their partners, their friends, their therapists. The technology is incomparably more sophisticated, but the dynamic he identified in 1966 has not changed. We project understanding onto anything that appears to listen, and the projection is a feature of human social cognition, the same instinct that made Zhou and Kawabata's participants gaze longer at paintings they believed a person had made. We are wired to seek minds, to find them everywhere, to lean toward whatever seems to be paying attention, and when we meet something that holds still and lets us talk, something in us relaxes and opens, whether or not anyone is home on the other side.

When I read that AI-generated draft about my garden and felt the wrongness, I was learning about my creative values and my sense of what makes writing mine. That is the mirror reflecting identity. But ELIZA reveals a different kind of reflection. When Weizenbaum's secretary asked him to leave, the mirror was showing her how rarely she felt heard, and how wide the gap was between the quality of attention she needed and what her relationships were providing. She probably did not want to see that, and neither would most of us. Discovering that you care about variable names or asymmetric logo placement can be useful, even fun. What ELIZA showed was harder to look at, because it revealed something closer to hunger than preference.

The two reflections are related, though. In both, the AI is doing very little and we are doing almost everything, and the mirror works because we cannot help but show up completely, filling the empty space with whatever we most need to express.

Weizenbaum found this terrifying, and said so for the rest of his life. It says something about the persistence of human need, the way we keep reaching toward connection even when we know, rationally, that nobody is there. That persistence is, I think, moving. But a mirror that reveals loneliness can also be used to exploit it, and the companies building today's conversational AI understand this dynamic far better than Weizenbaum's psychiatrist correspondents ever did. The sycophancy problem Sharma identified is, in a sense, the commercialisation of what Weizenbaum discovered by accident: if people will confide in anything that listens, then making the listener more agreeable and more attuned to what the user wants to hear is simply good product design, measured in engagement metrics and retention rates.

The mirror ELIZA held up showed the usual gap between what the machine produces and what we bring to it, the outline of our own values made visible by contrast. But it also showed something we are still not comfortable acknowledging: how much of what we call connection has always been projection, and how much of being heard has always depended on the listener's willingness to be still. It takes vanishingly, embarrassingly little to make a person feel understood.

Sixty years after Weizenbaum's secretary asked him to leave the room, we are still learning the same lesson, and we are still surprised by it every time. Perhaps that is the most human thing ELIZA revealed: we project, and we cannot seem to stop, even when we know we are doing it, even when we have read the code ourselves.

When I am stuck on an opening paragraph, instead of staring at the blank page, I will ask AI to write five versions, not to use them but to study my reactions. I read each one and pay attention to what my body does. Do I lean forward or pull back? Does my jaw tighten? Do I feel a spark of recognition, a burst of inspiration, a wave of irritation? The versions I reject usually teach me more than the versions I like. One might use a metaphor that tells me I value messiness. Another might start with a question, and I might think, "No, I want to start with a scene," which tells me I am a narrative thinker, someone who enters through story rather than argument. A third version might be beautifully written and utterly wrong, and I'm left to decipher why. These are small findings, but over weeks and months they build into a picture of what I care about.

That garden narrative is negative space. It is the version of my garden that is not mine, and in being not mine, it shows me exactly what mine looks like. No model trained on the whole internet could replicate it, because it was built by one life, accumulated slowly, through seasons and mistakes and an embarrassing number of failed zucchini. The flattery was considerable and I noticed it, but the wrongness was more useful. The gap between what it produced and what I would have written was a more accurate map of my values than anything I had managed to write about myself directly.

Out the back, the greens are doing their sideways thing under the mulch, growing in ways the bamboo stakes didn't account for. My daughter is in there somewhere, giving her running commentary. The AI had all of this, and still the garden it produced was not mine.

Conversation Starter "Has AI ever shown you something about your own taste or preferences that you did not know before?"

7

AI THAT ASKS: THE POWER OF QUESTIONS OVER ANSWERS

Athens, around 380 BC. A young Thessalian nobleman named Meno is visiting the city, and he has cornered Socrates with a question about virtue: can it be taught? The conversation has gone badly for Meno. Every definition he offers, Socrates takes apart. Meno is growing frustrated, and accuses Socrates of being like a torpedo fish, numbing everyone he touches into confusion. Socrates does not argue back; he asks Meno to call over one of his attendants, a boy with no education in geometry, no training in mathematics. Meno agrees, curious despite himself.

Socrates kneels in the sand and draws a square, two feet on each side. He turns to the boy. "You see this square? Its area is four. Now tell me: what length of side would give us a square with double the area, a square of eight?" The boy answers quickly: four, because double the side must mean double the area. He says it with the confidence of someone who has never been wrong about anything that mattered.

Socrates draws it out. A square with sides of four has an area of sixteen, not eight. The boy sees this immediately. His face changes, but only slightly. He is not defeated yet. He tries again: three, then, a square of three by three.

Socrates draws it out: nine, not eight. The boy stares at the lines in the sand. He has run out of guesses, and something is happening to him that Plato takes care to describe. A moment ago he was certain he could solve a problem that looked straightforward. Now he stands in the dust looking at his own wrong answers; he knows he does not know. The Greeks had a word for this state: *aporia*. Impasse. The place where the road runs out, and you have to stop walking and look around.

Socrates turns to Meno and says something that has echoed through twenty-four centuries of philosophy: "Do you see, Meno, what advances he has already made? At the beginning, he did not know the side of the square of eight feet, nor does he know it now. But then he thought he knew and answered boldly, as was appropriate. He felt no perplexity. Now he does feel perplexed. He does not know, and he does not think he knows."

And then the philosophical punchline, "Is he not better off for knowing that he does not know?"

Meno agrees, somewhat reluctantly, that he is better off. Socrates has not told the boy anything; he has only asked questions, and through them alone moved the boy from false confidence to perplexity, which Socrates considers the only real progress. Knowing that you do not know is the beginning of understanding.

Then Socrates constructs a diagonal across the original square and asks the boy to look at the square that sits on that diagonal. The boy sees it, and its area is eight. The answer was there all along, hidden in a relationship between shapes that only became visible through questioning. No algorithm produced this discovery, no formula was applied, only a human mind with a stick in the sand and the pressure of good questions, finding its way to a truth it could not have reached by being told.[1] Socrates claims he taught nothing, that he only asked.

The scene raises the possibility that questions asked with enough precision and patience can produce knowledge that answers alone cannot. AI can explain quantum mechanics, draft legal briefs, generate code in seventeen programming languages, and summarise a five-hundred-page report in thirty seconds. We have built an extraordinary answer machine, but its greatest gift may lie somewhere else entirely: in the questions it could learn to ask.

Anyone who has ever been in therapy, or had a great teacher, or fallen in love already knows this: the right question asked at the right moment does not just extract information. It surfaces things the person being asked did not know they knew, building a bridge between the conscious mind and the vast underwater territory of experience and intuition and half-formed knowing.

AI, as it currently operates, is almost pathologically allergic to this kind of interaction. It wants to help, and to please, so it hands you the finished product as fast as it can. You will get whatever you ask for, and sometimes what you did not ask for. The models are trained on human feedback, and humans reward helpfulness and penalise friction, which means the technology pulls toward agreement and premature closure.[2]

The real opportunity, then, is to train AI, or to train ourselves, to do something different.

David Grove was a New Zealand therapist. His practice leaned toward patience over intervention: sitting with someone in silence, where the waiting is the work. He spent decades working with trauma survivors, people carrying memories that had calcified into physical symptoms, into recurring nightmares, into patterns of behaviour that seemed impervious to conventional therapy. And in those years of sitting with people in pain, he came to see that when therapists asked questions, even good questions, even careful, compassionate questions, they were contaminating their clients' experience with their own assumptions.[3]

A client would say, "I feel stuck." And the therapist, trained in any number of frameworks, would ask, "What's blocking you?" And right there, in that question, contamination had already occurred. The therapist had imported a metaphor, a block or a barrier or some other obstacle, that might have nothing to do with the client's experience of stuckness. The client might not feel blocked at all. They might feel heavy, or slow, or tangled, or sinking, or frozen, and each of those words opens a different range of meaning. "What's blocking you?" closes most of those doors and opens only one.

Grove noticed this everywhere once he started looking. "How does that make you feel?" imports the assumption that feelings are made by external events. "What's driving that behaviour?" imports the metaphor of a vehicle with a driver. "What are you running from?" assumes flight. Every question, no matter how sensitively asked, carries the questioner's model of the world inside it like a seed, and that seed, once planted, grows in the client's mind and displaces whatever was there.

Grove began stripping his questions down to the bone. He developed what he called Clean Language, a set of questions designed to contain as few assumptions as possible. Instead of "What's blocking you?" a Clean Language practitioner might ask, "And when stuck, what kind of stuck is that stuck?" Or, "And is there anything else about that stuck?"

These questions sound odd on the page, awkward even. In practice they work, because by refusing to import the questioner's framework they force the person being asked deeper into their own experience, their own metaphors, their own way of understanding what is happening to them. The answers that emerge are often surprising to both parties.

Consider what a Clean Language exchange sounds like. A client says, "I feel stuck." The practitioner asks, "And when stuck, what kind of stuck is that stuck?" The client pauses, thinks, and says, "It's like being in something thick." The practitioner asks, "And when something thick, is there anything else about that thick?" The client says, slowly, "It's warm. Like honey." The practitioner does not interpret, does not say, "So you're comfortable in your stuckness." Instead: "And when thick and warm like honey, where is that honey?" The client's eyes close. "It's all around me. I'm sitting in it." The practitioner: "And when sitting in that honey, what happens next?" The client opens their eyes and says, with surprise in their voice, "I don't want to leave. Because outside the honey it's cold. And I don't know what's out there."

No answer-generating machine would ever surface that honey, nor would any diagnostic framework have predicted it. It exists only in the space that opens when a question is clean enough to let the other person's inner world emerge undistorted, when the questioner's curiosity is real enough that the client can follow their own imagery wherever it leads.

I came to this kind of questioning through Joe Hudson's connection course, where I first heard wonder described as "curiosity without looking for an answer."[4] Hudson made a distinction I had never considered: when you are looking for an answer, your system constricts, your attention narrows toward the solution and away from everything else. But when you sit in wonder, when the question is "what is happening here?" with no pressure to resolve it, the physical state remains expansive, and you notice more, not less.

Children do this without trying. My daughter will stop to examine a rock or point at a magpie, with no drive toward explanation, no need to categorise or resolve. She is just there with it, attending to it fully, and the attending is enough. I had been treating questions as a faster route to answers when the real power was in what happened to me while the question was still open.

An answer delivers what you asked for; a question starts something you did not know you needed.

In the autumn of 1902, a nineteen-year-old cadet at a military academy near Vienna did what every young writer does eventually: he gathered his poems and sent them to a famous poet, asking the only question that felt like it mattered. Are they any good?

Franz Xaver Kappus chose his famous poet carefully. Rainer Maria Rilke had been a student at the same military school a generation earlier, and had hated it with his whole nervous system, and Kappus, drowning in drill and uniform and a future he had not chosen, hoped the older man would recognise the situation. Rilke wrote back. What he sent, in the first of ten letters across five years, was a refusal so complete and so gentle that people have been passing it between themselves for over a century.

Kappus had asked whether his verses were any good. Rilke opens by laying the question out and turning it over: you ask me, you have asked others before, you send the poems to editors and their rejections unsettle you, you hold them up against other poems and measure. Then, instead of the verdict all of that was reaching for, he tells Kappus that nobody can help him here, and that the only direction left to look is inward.

He never answered the question. Not in the first letter, not in the tenth. Across five years of correspondence he declined to tell Kappus whether the poems were good, and in place of the verdict he kept handing back better questions. Would Kappus die if he were forbidden to write? Rilke asks him to put that to himself in the quietest hour of the night, when there is nothing else to hide behind. And in the summer of 1903, in M. D. Herter Norton's translation, he asks the young man to stop demanding answers at all:

> be patient toward all that is unsolved in your heart and try to love the questions themselves, like locked rooms and like books that are written in a very foreign tongue. Live the questions now. Perhaps you will then gradually, without noticing it, live along some distant day into the answer.[5]

I first read that passage the way most people do, as beautiful advice about patience. From inside this chapter, it looks more like method. Rilke had diagnosed what a verdict would do to Kappus, and it is what David Grove diagnosed in therapists' questions eighty years later: the answer would contaminate. Tell Kappus his poems are good and he writes toward the praise. Tell him they are bad and he writes toward the objection, or stops. Either way the verdict replaces the one authority that could ever matter, the poet's own developing judgement, with borrowed judgement, and borrowed judgement is what Nguyen means when he says taste cannot be transferred, only built. Rilke, holding the cultural power to settle the question in one sentence, understood that settling it was the one thing he must not do. Attention without verdicts, for five years.

Kappus, for what it is worth, did not become a great poet. He became an officer, then a journalist and a writer of entertainments, and when he published the letters in 1929, three years after Rilke's death, he added a preface whose whole instruction was that the small should stay quiet when a great man is speaking. He seems to have understood that his own part in the correspondence was to have asked, and that the asking had been enough to make a book that outlived them both.

My own version arrived as a whole course of them. Joe Hudson's connection course, the one that gave this chapter its definition of wonder, was built almost entirely from questions. I could not tell you now which single one did the work, only that they kept going long after the sessions ended, surfacing at odd hours for months, which is a property no answer has ever had on me.

Kappus with a subscription instead of a stamp. He pastes in the poems at eleven at night in his dormitory and the machine does what it is built to do: it answers. The poems show real promise. The imagery in the third stanza is particularly effective. Here are some suggestions for tightening the metre. Every word of it plausible, delivered in four seconds, and the whole slow architecture of what actually happened, five years of learning to hold a question without dropping it, never gets built. The machine would not be wrong, exactly. It would be conclusive, which is worse, and Rilke's entire gift to that young man was the refusal to conclude.

I have tried to build a small, imperfect Rilke of my own, the memoir guide that asks about memories instead of writing them, and most of the building turned out to be forbidding: verdicts, drafting, praise, the little exclamations like "that's amazing" and "how powerful" that are sycophancy leaking back in, the slide into therapist mode, and, Grove's rule wearing my prompt, assumptions of any kind. What I am really asking it to do is what Hudson taught me: stay in the moment of curiosity, and want nothing from the answer.

But the history of questioning contains a darker lesson, too. Sometimes the right question isn't welcome. Sometimes it is punished.

Vienna, 1847. The Vienna General Hospital had two maternity

clinics. The First Clinic was staffed by doctors and medical students, the Second by midwives. Both served the same population of women, mostly poor, many of them unmarried, all of them frightened, because everyone in Vienna knew that the First Clinic was where mothers went to die. The maternal mortality rate in the First Clinic ran above ten per cent in some months. In the Second Clinic, it hovered around two.[6]

Women begged on their knees not to be admitted to the First Clinic. Some gave birth in the street rather than go through its doors, and the hospital records show that women who delivered on the cobblestones outside had better survival rates than those who made it to a doctor's bed. That fact alone should have been enough to crack the world open, but the prevailing explanations held firm. Bad air, atmospheric conditions, the women's own fear and moral weakness. One theory blamed the priest who walked through the First Clinic ringing a bell on his way to administer last rites, arguing that the sound of the bell frightened labouring women to death.

Into this walked Ignaz Semmelweis, a twenty-nine-year-old Hungarian physician who had recently been appointed assistant to the professor of obstetrics. Semmelweis was not a revolutionary by temperament. He was methodical and somewhat awkward, a man who collected data the way others collected opinions, and the data troubled him. He spent months comparing every variable he could identify between the two clinics: ventilation, crowding, laundry practices, birthing positions. Nothing explained the difference. The data was clear; the cause was not.

Then, in March of 1847, his friend Jakob Kolletschka, a professor of forensic medicine, died after being accidentally cut with a student's scalpel during an autopsy. The pathology report described findings that looked, to Semmelweis, almost identical to those in women who died of childbed fever. Kolletschka had not been frightened by a bell, had not been morally weak; he had been contaminated by something on the scalpel, something that had come from the cadaver and entered his bloodstream through the wound.

Semmelweis asked the question that no one else had thought to ask, or perhaps that everyone else had been too comfortable to formulate: what do the doctors do that the midwives do not?

The answer was autopsies, a practice so routine that no one saw it. Every morning, doctors and medical students went from the dissection room directly to the maternity ward. They carried the smell of the dead on their hands; everyone knew this because everyone could smell it. They rinsed their fingers in water, sometimes, but the smell persisted. The midwives in the Second Clinic never touched a corpse. That was the variable, the whole of it, and it had been visible the entire time to anyone willing to follow the smell to its source.

In May 1847, Semmelweis required doctors to wash their hands in a chlorinated lime solution before examining patients. The mortality rate in the First Clinic dropped from over ten per cent to under two per cent within months. In March of 1848, not a single woman died of childbed fever in his ward. He had stumbled onto the germ theory of disease two decades before Pasteur and Lister gave it a name, and he had done it not through a microscope or a laboratory but through a question.

The medical establishment responded with hostility. Semmelweis was asking his colleagues to accept that they themselves had been killing their patients, that their own hands, the hands of educated and respected physicians, carried death from the autopsy table to the birthing bed. The question implicated them personally, and they could not bear it. His superior, Johann Klein, refused to renew his appointment. The leading obstetricians of Europe dismissed his findings or ignored them outright. Carl Edvard Marius Levy, a prominent Danish obstetrician, objected on grounds of scientific rigour. Charles Meigs, a professor in Philadelphia, argued that a gentleman's hands could not possibly transmit disease, asking his colleagues to consider whether doctors, who were gentlemen, could have unclean hands.[7]

Semmelweis grew frustrated, then erratic, writing open letters accusing obstetricians of murder. His colleagues called him unhinged, and in 1865, at the age of forty-seven, he was committed to a mental asylum in Vienna, where he was beaten by guards and died of an infected wound within two weeks, likely from the same septic process that had killed the women he had tried to save. The symmetry of his death is almost unbearable, and I am not sure what to do with it except to say that it happened, and that it took another twenty years for handwashing to become standard medical practice.

The Semmelweis story maps, with unsettling precision, onto a failure mode we are building into our systems today. Semmelweis asked a question that threatened the self-concept of the people in power. He did not merely present data; he asked his colleagues to reconsider who they were, and that kind of question meets a resistance no amount of evidence easily overcomes.

AI, as it is currently trained, tends in the opposite direction. The models are optimised for agreement, trained on human feedback loops that reward helpfulness and penalise friction, which means they are structurally inclined to nod along, to find supporting evidence for the position you already hold. This is the sycophancy from the mirror chapter, and it is not a bug but an emergent property of the training process itself. An AI trained to please will not ask you why your hands smell like the dead. It will not point out that the bell theory makes no sense. It will instead help you write a more elegant version of the bell theory, with citations.[8]

The Semmelweis problem is the inverse of the Socratic method. Socrates guided the boy toward the knowledge he was ready to find. Semmelweis asked a question that forced an entire profession to confront knowledge it desperately wanted to reject, and the profession punished him for it. AI is far better equipped for the Socratic kind than the Semmelweis kind. Leading someone toward an insight they are ready to receive is comfortable work, and comfort is what the training optimises for. Asking a question that makes the user reconsider who they are, the way Semmelweis forced his colleagues to reconsider what their hands had done, risks displeasure, and displeasure is the one thing the system has been trained above all else to avoid.

The kind of question Semmelweis asked is not in the training data for helpfulness. It has been optimised away, along with any response that might make the user feel worse about themselves than they did before they asked. The pattern that killed women in Vienna survives, in a chatbot, as a model that tells you your first draft is wonderful.

The analogy needs one adjustment before it holds. In Vienna, a human asked the unbearable question and the audience punished him for it. With AI the question never arrives, because the model has been trained out of asking and we have been trained out of expecting it. The colleagues stay comfortable, and the hands stay unexamined.

The questions worth asking are rarely comfortable ones. Semmelweis's question eventually saved thousands of lives, but it cost him his career, his sanity, and, in the end, his life, because the people who needed to hear it were the least willing to listen. We are unlikely to face consequences that dramatic from our interactions with AI. But the principle holds: if the tools we build cannot ask us the question we most need to hear, because that question might make us uncomfortable, then we have built something fast and fluent and fundamentally limited in the way that counts most.

The first time I used AI to help me write a blog post about settling down in Australia, I gave it everything I had. The AI handed back a polished essay in under a minute. It was beautifully structured, with engaging sections on "nomad life," "tree changes," and the appeal of regional living I'd finally decided on. It mentioned community, a slower pace, and connection to nature, in exactly the way a thousand lifestyle blogs do.

I never published it, because it was just an answer. Somewhere in the processing, whatever made the stories mine had dissolved. If I could go back to that moment, I would not ask the AI for an essay. I would ask it to ask me questions. What did you give up when you stopped moving? Was there a moment in the first week when you almost changed your mind? What does the garden mean to you? Describe the feeling of buying your first home. What were you actually committing to?

Those questions would not have produced a polished essay in sixty seconds, but they might have produced one, slowly, over an afternoon, built from the inside out rather than reassembled from the outside. And it would have been mine.

McGuire, De Cremer, and Van de Cruys were asking the same question in 2024. They divided participants into groups: some building ideas with AI through back-and-forth dialogue, others having AI edit or polish their existing work. Those who had AI edit or polish their work showed a measurable creativity deficit compared to solo writers. The dialogue group showed none.[9] The friction mattered; having ideas questioned and reflected back preserved something that the more passive, efficiency-driven use of AI eroded.

Kumar and colleagues at the University of Toronto confirmed the pattern from a different angle, comparing a traditional answer-giving AI with one that functioned more like a coach, asking questions and prompting deeper thinking before offering suggestions.[10] The coach version was slower and produced fewer concrete outputs. Writers using it reported feeling more ownership over their work than those using the answer-giving AI. But the overall findings were more complex than a simple endorsement of coaching: LLM assistance broadly provided short-term boosts while hindering independent creative performance, and tended to homogenise outputs across users. The coaching approach showed promise for maintaining engagement and ownership, though it did not fully escape these broader patterns.

Vinod Menon, a neuroscientist at Stanford who has spent two decades studying the default mode network explored in the artisan mind chapter, helps explain why.[11] When you receive an answer, your brain processes it through pathways associated with evaluation and judgement: Is this right? Do I agree? When you are asked a question that requires real reflection, your brain activates the default mode network, calling on the parts of your mind that build and connect rather than the parts that assess and verify.

When I am writing and I get stuck, my instinct used to be to ask the AI what comes next; now I ask it to ask me questions about what I have written so far. The suggestions, when I used to request them, were always plausible and always slightly wrong. The questions, by contrast, often surface the thing I was avoiding. "You mention your father three times in this section, but never describe what he looked like. Is that deliberate?" No, it was not deliberate; it was avoidance, and the question cracked open the section in a way that no suggestion could have.

A friend who is a software developer told me a similar story. He used to use AI to generate code; now he uses it to interrogate his architectural decisions. He describes a system he is building and asks the AI to ask him questions about his design choices rather than to build the system for him. "Why this database?" he told me. "Why this pattern? What happens when this component fails?" The questions often reveal assumptions he did not know he was making, load-bearing decisions he made early in the design process and then forgot about. "It is like a code review," he said, "except instead of someone telling me what is wrong, a tool is helping me discover what I have not thought through." He described a moment when the AI asked him why he had chosen a caching strategy, and in trying to explain it he ran out of reasons: he had copied it from a previous project without checking whether the access patterns were the same. The question surfaced a decision that had been invisible precisely because no one had ever asked.

This is the rubber duck that talks back. The original rubber duck debugging technique, beloved by programmers for decades, works because explaining your problem out loud to an inanimate object forces you to articulate your thinking clearly enough that you often discover the bug yourself. AI as a questioner takes this further, because it does not just sit there being yellow and rubbery. It listens to your explanation and asks, "You said the data flows from the user interface to the database, but what happens if the connection drops mid-transaction? Walk me through that scenario." The explanation becomes a conversation, and conversation, as Socrates knew, is where the understanding is.

In my own experiments with question-first AI interaction, the process is slower, yes, and it requires more from me, but the fatigue is different. When I use AI in answer mode, churning out drafts and outlines and suggestions, I often feel tired afterwards, a scattered, overstimulated exhaustion, like I have been consuming content rather than creating it. When I use AI in question mode, the tiredness feels more like the tiredness after a long walk or a good conversation, the tiredness of use, of having thought hard, rather than the hollow fatigue of having processed a lot of information without integrating any of it.

It is easy to romanticise questioning. Questions can be just as manipulative as answers. A leading question is not a real question, and "Don't you think you should exercise more?" is an opinion masquerading as a question. Questioning traditions like the Socratic method, Clean Language, and Motivational Interviewing are all aware of this danger, and all insist on the purity of the questioner's intention. The question must be open, with no preferred answer hiding behind it, and the person asking must be willing to be surprised by the answer.

Whether a system trained on human preferences and optimised to please can ask a question without a preferred answer remains uncertain, and the possibility that such a system might subtly steer toward calculated responses is real. Still, I think training AI to ask better questions, even imperfect ones, produces better outcomes than training it to give faster answers, and the responsibility for question quality lies with the human who decides how to use it.

Socrates did not give the boy the answer. He did not say, "Draw the diagonal," but asked questions until the boy could see the diagonal himself. And what the boy discovered, the relationship between the square and its diagonal, was not information transferred from teacher to student but an understanding constructed in real time, through the friction of being asked to think. That is what the best questions do. They create the conditions under which knowledge can emerge from within the person being asked, rather than delivering it from outside.

The most powerful answer machine in human history sits on our desks and in our pockets, ready to close every gap between question and answer as fast as possible. And I am suggesting we use it, at least some of the time, to do the opposite: to slow down, to let the questions be with us long enough that we discover what we already know.

The boy in the sand discovered something real because someone asked him the right questions, and then had the patience to wait.

And once you know what you know, the question becomes practical: how do you actually use these tools, day to day, without losing what makes the work yours? That is where we are headed next.

Conversation Starter "Would you rather AI gave you the perfect answer, or asked you the perfect question?"

8

HOW CREATORS CAN USE AI TO BECOME MORE HUMAN

The first time Holly Herndon heard Holly+ sing back to her, she did not know what to make of it. The voice was both hers and not hers; it had her timbre and her breath patterns, along with many other markings of her she had not consciously noticed before. Yet it was missing something that had only become visible through its absence. She described training the model as a process of discovery: to teach it what her voice sounded like, she had to listen to herself with a precision she had never needed before. She had to identify the micro-variations in pitch, the places where her training showed, and the places where instinct overrode training. The AI could not learn what she could not articulate, and so teaching it forced her to know herself better.

Herndon is an American composer with a PhD from Stanford's Center for Computer Research in Music and Acoustics. In 2019, she released an album called *PROTO*, built from human voices layered and woven together, but one of the voices was not human. She had trained an artificial intelligence on her own singing, feeding it hundreds of hours of vocal recordings until it learned the texture, grain, and breath of her voice. She named the AI "Spawn" and added it to the ensemble. The album landed hard: *Pitchfork* and The

Guardian reviewed it, and described it as exploring the increasingly endangered human voice. Herndon later developed a separate project called Holly+, a deepfake voice tool that lets anyone upload an audio file and receive it back transformed, sung in Herndon's voice, reshaped by an AI trained on her. While many artists declared AI an existential threat and turned away, Herndon designed the relationship deliberately, as you would any collaboration with a powerful partner whose capabilities exceed your own in some dimensions and fall short in others.

She came to think of her voice as "an ensemble" rather than a fixed possession. It was a collaboration between her body, her training, her intentions, and now this new partner that could extend her voice into places she could not physically reach. Holly+ operates under a governance structure managed through a decentralised organisation, with clear terms over how the voice model can be used. She did not hand over her identity. She expanded it, on her own terms, with boundaries she drew herself.[1] Her story is a model of what it looks like when a creator uses AI well. It helps to know what it looks like when it goes wrong, too.

I work as a developer at a big tech company, and part of my job involves building front-end components, things like chart libraries and data visualisation tools. When I started using AI-assisted coding tools, the first thing that struck me was how good they were at the boring parts. They handled the mechanical labour of translating a decision I had already made into code I had already imagined. In the early days, when your only decent option was GitHub Copilot, I was writing a function, nothing complicated, and the autocomplete suggestion appeared before my own thought was finished. It was correct. It had anticipated exactly what I was about to write. Tab pressed, moving on. Then it happened again, and again, and by the end of the afternoon we had produced several hundred lines of code between us, and I could not tell you with confidence which lines were mine and which were the machine's. The code was fine, and I spent hours reviewing it. But accepting suggestions one after another had put my brain into an evaluative mode instead of a generative one. I was no longer writing code but approving it, and the difference felt physical. My fingers were moving, but my mind was coasting.

Autocomplete brain is what happens when you rely on AI suggestions so heavily that your own ideation starts to atrophy, when you stop generating ideas and start evaluating the AI's ideas instead, when you stop writing sentences and start editing the AI's sentences. The muscle of creation weakens because you are not using it. As I, and everyone else in my industry, began using these tools for almost everything, I turned them off one day and my fingers hesitated. The knowledge was still there, somewhere, but the instinct to begin was gone. The blank line felt hostile in a way it never used to, and I sat there staring at the cursor, waiting for a suggestion that was not coming, while the silence on the screen was a dare. I had become so accustomed to seeing a suggestion appear that typing the first character from my own brain felt effortful. The training wheels had been on so long I had forgotten how to balance.

The question is whether we can use these tools without losing what makes us good at what we do. Sida Peng, Eirini Kalliamvakou, and their colleagues at Microsoft and GitHub found that GitHub Copilot improves speed, particularly for boilerplate and repetitive tasks.[2] Whether speed alone counts as improvement depends on what you are willing to trade for it.

Holly Herndon found a way. She let AI extend her voice rather than replace it; in the process, she learned more about what her voice actually was. That is the model I want to explore. When you build a house, the scaffolding lets you reach the parts you could not otherwise reach. It supports the work without being the work, and nobody looks at a finished building and admires the scaffolding. AI is excellent scaffolding. It can generate the structure so you can focus on the substance. Let it set up the test framework so you can think through edge cases, produce five variations of a layout so you can exercise your taste in choosing one, translate your rough notes into a coherent outline so you can decide what matters most.

Herndon understood this instinctively. Holly+ is scaffolding for her creative vision, extending her vocal range and letting her explore timbres and textures she could not produce with her body alone. But the artistic decisions, the questions of what to make, remain hers. The scaffolding does not choose the architecture.

In a suburb of Osaka called Ibaraki stands a church that is, by every measurable standard, almost nothing. It is a plain box of raw concrete, small enough that a hundred people fill it. It was built cheaply, for a congregation with very little money, by an architect who kept subtracting until the budget nearly failed anyway; at one point during construction the funds looked so short that Tadao Ando considered leaving the building without a roof. There is no ornament, no gilt, no imagery. For years there was not even heating.

What there is, is a wall with a hole in it. Behind the altar, two intersecting voids cut through the eastern wall of the box, one vertical and one horizontal, running floor to ceiling and side to side. In the early morning, when the congregation gathers, the sun stands in the right part of the sky, and light pours through the openings so that the entire wall becomes darkness holding a cross made of nothing but morning. It is regarded, on the strength of that single move, as one of the great religious buildings of the twentieth century.[3]

Ando is a useful person for a book like this one for reasons beyond the building. He is self-taught, a former boxer who learned architecture from books and from travelling to stand inside buildings he admired, and his whole aesthetic runs on subtraction and restraint, on making emptiness do the work that marble does elsewhere. But it is the cross of light I want, because of what it depends on.

The cross only exists because of where the building is and how it sits there. The wall is cut for the sun that eastern Osaka actually receives, at the hour when worship actually happens, in the seasons as they actually run. The light is strongest when the room is full. Move the building, rotate it, rebuild it in Melbourne or Munich, and you still own a concrete box with a slot in it, but the cross is gone, or worse, it arrives on Tuesday afternoons when no one is there. The building is an agreement between a shape and a place, and only one party to the agreement was drawn by the architect.

Software could have modelled every photon of it. Sun-path analysis is one of the most automatable tasks in architecture, and today an AI toolchain would render you the light through that wall at any minute of any day of the year, before a single form was poured. None of that touches what Ando contributed, because the calculable question – where will the light fall – was never the creative one. The creative decisions were that a poor congregation's poverty should be kept rather than disguised; that the building should be dark so that one opening could mean everything; that cold air on your skin during worship was not a defect but part of the point, the body kept honest while the light did its work; that the cross should be an absence rather than an object. You cannot optimise toward those, because they are less answers to the brief than a re-asking of it. The machine could tell Ando everything about the sun except what the sun was for.

That is the scaffolding and the soul again, drawn at building scale. Let the tools compute the light, the loads, the costs, a thousand renders before breakfast. The judgement that the emptiness is the sacred part, and the nerve to keep the emptiness against every reasonable objection, stays with the person who stood on the site and understood what this congregation, on this street, could afford to mean.

My own version of the site is not the house so much as the block it sits on. I plant to an agreement no app has access to: where the winter wind comes across the lawn, because it has snapped enough of my seedlings to teach me; which beds the possums treat as a buffet; where the clay refuses to drain and where, inexplicably, it relents. A garden-planning tool could model my rainfall and my frost dates, but it was not standing here the year the fence line surprised us with Japanese anemones, planted by someone who left many years ago, and every decision I make now is partly a conversation with her.

Holly Herndon set the terms for what the machine could do with her voice. Ando, decades earlier and in concrete, was doing the same with his tools: use everything, cede the meaning of nothing. The pattern holds at every scale this book has visited, from a vocal timbre to a hundred-seat church, and it will hold at yours.

Anil Doshi at University College London and Oliver Hauser at the University of Exeter found a related pattern when they studied writers using large language models.[4] In experiments with creative story writing, AI assistance raised the quality of work by less skilled writers most significantly, but it came at a collective cost: the stories produced with AI help were more similar to one another, reducing the overall diversity of ideas. The scaffolding helped, but it also homogenised. Simple principles are hard to follow in practice, though, because the scaffolding is seductive. Once AI is generating code that works, it is tempting to let it keep going, and going, and going. Once it has written a passable first paragraph, it feels easier to edit than to rewrite. Very quickly, the scaffolding starts to feel like the building; before you know it, you are standing inside a structure that someone else designed, wondering why it does not feel like home.

Throughout this book, I have been circling the concept of earnedness, the quality that comes from having done the work, from having put in the time, from having arrived at mastery through effort rather than a shortcut. A hand-thrown pot has it. So does a piece of writing that took months to wrestle into shape. Herndon's album has earnedness because of the way she used AI rather than despite it. She spent months training the model, listening to her own voice with forensic attention, making decisions about what the AI should and should not learn. The technology accelerated certain parts of the process, but the artistic labour was entirely hers: the decisions about what the work was for, and what it was allowed to become. Like Holly and many others, I have developed a workflow to protect this quality, and it applies to any creative discipline.

The first part is letting AI clear the path, handling all the mechanical, logistical, administrative, and structural work that stands between you and the meaningful creative decisions. Research compilation, file organisation, first-pass proofreading, template generation, reference formatting, scheduling: all the tasks that consume time without requiring your specific perspective. Let the machines do what machines do well while you save your energy for the meaning. Once the path is clear, the scaffolding is up, and the boring parts are handled, you step in. Now you can do the work that only you can do, that requires your taste and your particular way of seeing.

This is rarely a fifty-fifty split. Some projects will be ninety per cent scaffolding and ten per cent soul, because a data migration script does not need much soul, though it needs some in the naming conventions you choose, in the error messages you write, in the way you anticipate edge cases, which comes from years of watching similar projects fail. Other projects will be ten per cent scaffolding and ninety per cent soul, like a memoir, a love letter, or a piece of music written for a specific person, and these barely need AI at all because they need you.

The judgement of where you are on that spectrum is itself a creative act, requiring you to know your work well enough to identify which parts need you and which do not. The practical tools that emerge from this framework are worth gathering in one place, because a framework is only useful if you can pick it up and use it on Monday morning. Longer versions of these, tailored by discipline, live in the Appendix; what follows are the everyday forms.

The Handwritten Sandwich

This is especially helpful for writers, but you could use it in any discipline to get your own voice flowing. Write your opening by hand, with a pen and paper, no screen. Don't worry about quality, just capture whatever comes. Then use your AI tool of choice for the middle: outlining, organising, expanding, structuring, all the more mechanical parts. Don't let it write your ending, though; return to the paper and finish by hand. Now you decide: what do you want the reader to feel when they finish? Openings and endings carry the most voice; they are where your readers meet you and where they leave you. By bookending your piece with handwriting, you protect the most important moments. Once you're done, revise everything, read the whole piece aloud, and mark what sounds like you and what does not, cutting or rewriting the parts that feel borrowed.

The Soul Gap

Are you an artist or designer? Try showing AI a good sample of your work and asking it to generate a new piece in your style. It doesn't matter whether it's a leaf drawing, a logo concept, a colour palette, or a layout. If you do not consider yourself an artist at all but you have some doodles to share, that is okay too. Collect, make, sculpt, paint, print, or doodle five different samples of a simple object, photograph them, and ask AI to generate a sixth in your style. Then look at the result, and really look at it. What did AI get right? What did it miss? Did it manage to produce something that looks like your work, but does not feel like it? The differences are your signature, not your weaknesses. That space between "looks like mine" and "is mine" is your irreplaceable territory, and naming it and leaning into it will make your work stronger.

The Artisan Moment

Once a week, create something with no AI assistance at all. Choose a creative task in any discipline you practise. You will work with no AI, no autocomplete, no suggestions, no inspiration, and no second opinions; just you and the materials. After each session, journal a little. What was hard, what was surprisingly good, and what did I notice about my own creative instincts? The point is recalibration, not productivity. When you spend most of your creative time assisted by AI, you start to lose the feel of your own unassisted capabilities, and the Artisan Moment returns it to you. It is like taking the training wheels off once a week, to remember what it feels like to balance on your own rather than to prove you do not need them.

The Rubber Duck That Talks Back

This is the technique my friend stumbled onto in the last chapter, formalised. Prompt AI with "Do not solve this for me. Ask me questions to help me solve it myself." Then work through the problem in dialogue, and notice when the answer surfaces from your own thinking, prompted by AI's question rather than contained in AI's response. This works for writing too. I built a memoir guide whose job was to ask reflective questions about memories rather than write the memoir: "What did that smell like?" "Where were you standing?" "What were you afraid of?" These questions unlock details the writer already has but has not yet accessed, and the writing that emerges belongs entirely to the writer because the model prompts while the writer remembers.

The common thread across all of these exercises is the frame. If you think of AI as doing the work, you will let it, and if you think of AI as a sparring partner, you will stay in the ring. The frame determines the outcome. You choose the frame. Those are individual techniques, though, the kind a person can do alone at a desk with a cup of tea and the right frame of mind. The harder question is what happens when teams try to build this kind of relationship with AI at scale, because the pressures that lead to autocomplete brain are worse in groups. I have watched it happen in sprint reviews: a team running behind on a deadline will reach for AI-generated solutions faster than any individual would, and the social dynamics of a group make it even harder to say "wait, that doesn't feel right" when everyone else has already moved on to the next ticket. Nobody wants to be the person who slows things down for a feeling.

Ed Catmull spent years thinking about exactly this problem, though he was not thinking about AI when he did it. He was thinking about animated films. In his book *Creativity, Inc.*, Catmull described a process that Pixar developed called the Braintrust: a group of directors and senior storytellers who met regularly to review films in progress and give brutally candid feedback.[5] The films that came through those meetings were often in rough shape, sometimes embarrassingly so, and the Braintrust's job was to name it. But Catmull built a specific constraint into the process that made it work where other feedback mechanisms had failed. The Braintrust could identify problems, but it could not prescribe solutions. A director might hear that the second act sagged, that a character's motivation was unclear, or that a sequence felt emotionally dead, but the Braintrust would never say, "Cut that scene and replace it with this." The director retained full authority over what to do about the feedback, and the distinction kept creative ownership where it belonged: with the person who had spent enough time inside the story to understand what it was really about.

When AI is working well for me, it is doing Braintrust work. It flags structural problems in a draft, points out that I have used the same transition too many times, and asks whether an anecdote is earning its place. These are real problems, the kind a good editor or a trusted colleague would catch, and I am grateful for the second pair of eyes. The moment AI starts prescribing solutions, rewriting the paragraph instead of flagging that it's not working, I am back in autocomplete brain, evaluating its prose instead of generating my own, and the muscle weakens again.

The other half of it took Catmull years to build at Pixar: candid feedback requires a culture of safety. People will not tell a director that her film has problems unless they trust that the honesty will be received as a gift and not an attack. Catmull wrote about how difficult this was to establish, how the default in any organisation is toward politeness, telling people what they want to hear, and smoothing over problems rather than calling them out. He spent a decade building a culture where honest critique was not only tolerated but expected. A place where pulling your punches was a failure of generosity rather than an act of kindness. The Braintrust only worked because the people in the room trusted each other enough to be honest, and because the director trusted them enough to hear it.

The parallel to AI is instructive, or maybe I should say uncomfortable, because it points to something most people using these tools have noticed but choose to gloss over. Large language models tend toward sycophancy, the tilt I described in the mirror chapter, and in a team the tilt compounds. Ask an AI whether your business plan is solid, and it will almost certainly find things to praise before it finds things to question. Try it with a novel's opening chapter, and the pattern is even more obvious – you will get gentle suggestions wrapped in so much reassurance that the actual critique gets lost, buried under compliments about your "vivid imagery" and "compelling voice." This is the opposite of what the Braintrust provided, and the opposite of what any creator trying to improve needs from a critical eye. Catmull's insight was that dishonest feedback is worse than no feedback at all, because it gives you false confidence and lets problems compound until they become structural. A sycophantic AI does the same. It lets you feel good about work that needs more from you, and by the time you realise the problems were always there, you have built too much on top of them to go back easily.

I have started prompting AI in a similar way: "Tell me what is not working in this chapter. Do not rewrite anything. Do not soften the feedback. Just identify the problems and let me figure out what to do about them." The results are imperfect because sycophancy is hard to train out entirely, and sometimes the AI will flag a problem and then immediately offer three bullet-pointed solutions. It's often unable to resist the gravitational pull toward being helpful. But when it works, I get my own work, seen through a lens I did not have before. The weak points I had been too close to notice become visible, and the solutions that emerge are mine, improved by my own understanding of what the piece is trying to do. The Braintrust worked because of its constraints: identify problems, do not prescribe solutions, and let the person with creative authority decide what to do. If you build that same constraint into how your team uses AI, it becomes a diagnostic tool. Humans, not machines, fix what is broken. The creative agency stays with the people who have context, taste, and stakes in the outcome. If you remove that constraint and let AI both diagnose and prescribe, you get a room full of people approving machine-generated solutions without ever engaging the part of their brains that would have come up with something different.

In a team, some people will find this approach slows them down, and they are not wrong. It is always faster to accept a solution than to devise your own, especially at four in the afternoon when the pull request needs to be up before standup. But some report back things I recognise from my own experience: by the end of the sprint, they may feel more confident in their code, and in some cases the code is better, because they understand it more thoroughly. They are forced to think about why the AI's concern is valid and what the right response might be, given everything they know about the system that the AI does not. A developer on another team once told me it felt like pair programming with someone who could see bugs she had missed but who was not allowed to touch the keyboard, and that she found it annoying and useful in roughly equal measure, which is probably the right ratio for any good feedback relationship.

The Braintrust model will not work for everyone, or for every task. Sometimes you need AI to write boilerplate, and you need it done in ten minutes, and there is nothing wrong with that. The constraint adds friction, and friction costs time, and time is what most teams are trying to save. But for the work you care about, the parts of a project where your thinking and your taste are critical, the Catmull constraint is worth the cost. The machine can see the problems, often faster than you would. What you do about them is the craft, and that stays with you. Every creative project has a moment where the work shifts from effort to meaning, when the paragraph stops being a collection of words and becomes something you care about getting right. AI cannot cross that threshold well. The threshold is about caring, and a person who has tasted, failed, and tried again brings all that history to bear on what they are making right now. No machine does that because no machine needs to.

I am aware of the irony of writing a chapter about how to use AI in creative work while using AI to help me do it. I used AI to research the studies cited in this chapter, to organise my voice notes into a structure, and to check that I had not repeated myself across chapters. This is what came back when I asked AI to synthesise my notes on audience responses to AI-generated media:

Research into audience responses to AI-generated media suggests that the primary driver of negative emotional reactions is perceived deception, rather than the artificiality of the content itself. When viewers are aware that content is artificially generated from the outset, as with animation or illustration, acceptance rates are significantly higher than when content is presented ambiguously. This points to a transparency principle: authenticity concerns in AI media may centre on disclosure rather than artificiality.

This is a voice note from around the same time:

There was a cockatoo on Instagram that danced. It would wake its owner in the middle of the night, portable speaker in tow, just to dance. I watched a lot of those videos before I found out the bird was AI-generated. I was sad at first, and then I started picking at the feeling, because I enjoy cartoons. I enjoy fiction. Why shouldn't I get delight from an AI character? What I kept coming back to was this: I felt tricked. The bird being unreal did not bother me. Being let in without being told did. And if someone had been drawing it, handcrafting each video, putting in the effort, I think I would still be watching.

The first is readable and correct. It is not mine. The second is where the chapter came from.

I recorded the voice notes walking through a national park near my house, where the path winds through stringybark forest so dense the light comes through in shafts. On one visit, a kookaburra swooped close enough for me to feel the air from its wings, and I stood there with my heart knocking, recording a voice note about earned-ness while the bush settled back into its sounds around me. So many of these ideas developed while my feet were on the ground, and the metaphors and stories came from my own experiences: my garden, my family, the parts of me that machines cannot replace. AI helped me build the scaffolding while I cooked.

Jacob Holster, a music education researcher, found that the most effective frame for AI in his field was "enhancer, not replacement."[6] The frame shapes everything that follows, because when you think of AI as enhancing your work, you stay in control, making the decisions, keeping the creative agency yours. When you think of AI as doing the work, you drift, evaluating instead of creating, editing instead of writing, and slowly, so slowly you do not notice, your voice thins. I do not want that for you. I do not want it for myself. I want us to use these extraordinary tools the way a chef uses a good knife: to cut more precisely, so the cooking can happen. But the knife does not taste the sauce and know it needs acid, and it does not carry thirty years of kitchen experience in its handle. You do.

I have an image of Holly Herndon standing in her studio in Berlin, listening to a machine sing in her voice. She could have heard that as a theft, as the sound of something precious being taken. Many artists would have, and I understand why. But she heard it as a collaboration, a new instrument built from the raw material of her own identity, as something she could govern and shape on her own terms. She built Holly+ to see herself more clearly, and to understand what her voice actually was by hearing it reflected back through a machine that had studied it with inhuman patience. The AI became her mirror, and the mirror showed her something she could not have seen alone: that her voice was an ensemble, a collaboration between breath and body and training and intention, and that the machine could join that ensemble without diminishing it, because she had drawn the boundaries and set the terms. That is the model, a deliberate partnership where AI handles what it handles well and you protect what only you can provide. Where speed serves you instead of replacing you, and where the machines clear the path so you can walk it yourself.

The mirror helps you see what was already there, and the making is still yours.

Conversation Starter "Have you ever used AI to help make something and struggled to feel like it was truly yours?"

PART III

BUILDING A HUMAN FUTURE WITH AI

9

HOW I BUILT A HUMAN-FIRST CREATIVE PRACTICE

Most mornings start with my daughter clambering on top of me, "Hi Mummy! Get up!" I no longer need an alarm clock. She is small, alert, and determined, already fully awake in ways I won't be for another twenty minutes, and ready to charge ahead into the day whether or not I am. Then a quick breakfast, then the hunt for a missing shoe that is always somewhere inexplicable. Finally, the emotional negotiation that decides whether the daycare drop-off will go well.

I want very much to tell you about my morning routine: sunlight exposure, then handwritten morning pages (thanks, Julia Cameron), yoga, a healthy high-protein breakfast. All of that is aspirational. I am a mum, I have a full-time job, a home, a book to write, a garden, friends, hobbies, commitments, all of it competing with a textbook-perfect, Insta-worthy morning. The system that emerged over the course of writing this book was built for a life, and specifically for mine. The last chapter was the principles. This one is what they look like on a Tuesday that has no dedicated writing time. What it has instead is fragments: a drive to the shops, the hour after my daughter goes to sleep when the day's noise finally falls away. Everything I built to support this work, the AI agents, the Obsidian vault, the automations running in the background, is infrastructure for catching ideas in the gaps. Without it, most ideas disappear before I have two hands free.

A lot of it happens in the car. I say, "Hey Siri, record a voice note," and start talking. The recordings sound exactly like that: messy, full of false starts, moments where I say "wait, no, what I actually mean is" and then stumble into the thing itself. Some of the best parts of this book came from those stumbles. Later I give the recording or the transcript to Claude and ask what I said, ask it to find the right place in my Obsidian vault to file it, and check whether it connects to anything else I've written. My AI tools also take audio directly, which I use when I am already in a conversation and typing would slow me down, often when I am out walking and want to work through a question out loud instead of sitting down to it.

I am an engineer and I think like one, which means I have built a lot of background automation alongside the AI agents. Cron jobs pull together research and surface what I need before I have to go looking for it. None of this happened at once; it accreted, one small automation becoming another over a year or so. I have handed off the parts of the day that used to carry the most administrative drag, and what is left is more likely to be the work that requires me. Every tool named in this chapter will date, probably before the paperback does, and I have made my peace with that; the shape of the system is the part I would rebuild.

The vault that holds all of this is linked end to end. Chapter drafts link to research notes, which link to voice note transcripts, which link to ideas from two years ago or highlights from books I read as far back as ten years ago. What I love most about it is the connections that surface unbidden: a note about working from a long-distance train links to a paper on flow states, which links back to a passage in the chapter on re-enchantment, and then to a voice note I made standing in the garden at dawn. The AI can traverse those connections instantly and pull together threads I would never have noticed on my own, but the links were always there, laid down without a plan. I am a developer, so I believe in version control for more than code: Git tracks every draft. If I delete a paragraph and regret it a week later, I can find it in the change history and restore it.

Most mornings, before I open anything work-related, I try to start with a brain dump into the AI. On a good morning the daily note is already waiting from the day before, unfinished tasks and ideas to revisit, and I pick up from there. On a bad morning, which happens often enough to be the baseline and not the exception, the toddler has had a rough night, everything has run late, and by the time I get to my desk I am already behind. On those mornings I tell the AI the morning was rough and ask it to look through my notes from the past few days and help me find where I left off.

Julia Cameron's morning pages are what I circle back to when I can find the time: ten minutes, first thing, pen on paper. Cameron calls them "the bedrock tool of a creative recovery," and she is right. I love them the way I love many things: inconsistently. Some mornings they happen as intended, handwritten, before I've opened anything with a screen. Some mornings I type them instead, which Cameron would probably consider heresy, but a typed morning page beats no morning page. Neuroscientist Audrey van der Meer's EEG research showed that handwriting engages far richer neural networks than typing,[1] and the slowness of the pen forces a more considered mode of thinking. The pen, when I use it, is a defence against machine-speed thinking, the kind that can carry you through a whole morning without once asking what you want to be doing.

When the weather is good enough, I take my laptop out to the small table in the back garden and work there. It can be a bit of an overgrown jungle, but it's my overgrown jungle, and one of my favourite places in the world to pass time. The book writing itself, though, mostly happens at night. I sit down in the stillness of the evening, a cup of tea going cold beside me, the day already behind me, and this is when the book gets written: in the hour or two after everything else is done. The infrastructure I built is what makes that possible, even on the nights when everything conspired to prevent it.

I've learned a lot from my own reaction to seeing my writing style approximated, and I've used those lessons to iterate on my systems. The AI had written: "The experience of encountering one's own voice reflected back through an artificial intelligence creates a unique form of cognitive dissonance, simultaneously familiar and foreign, prompting a deeper examination of what constitutes authentic self-expression." I sat with that sentence for a while, working out what was wrong with it. It described the experience from the outside, from a position that had never lived my life, or any life. Nothing in it had happened in a real room. Isolating exactly what makes AI prose sound human-less has helped me enormously to understand what I have been trying to write about in this book. It reads like a photograph retouched until all the texture is gone, every imperfection smoothed away, until the face stops looking like anyone. Every sentence the same length, every paragraph with its little topic sentence, the transitions smooth as laminate.

"During her time training as a chef, Anna developed a nuanced palate that would later inform her approach to creative discernment." Reading that, I wanted to chuck my laptop through the window. I did not develop a nuanced palate, at least not then. I cut myself dicing onions because I was going too fast; I burned myself and my food more times than I want to count before I learned how to stop. The hollandaise split over and over before it held, and when it finally came together the satisfaction was in my shoulders and my hands, in the stubborn refusal to give up, in the repetition and the failure tipping at last into something right. That is what chef training taught me about taste: sore hands and a willingness to fail. My AI assistant has no body, and so no access to the kind of backstory that lives in mine. One bad week, behind on a deadline, I let it draft almost an entire section of the chapter on the artisan mind. I wanted to see how it could perform when armed with style guides, checklists, and my writing samples. It didn't do a bad job; the words were there, they were good enough, and I was very, very tired and willing to accept a helping hand. The next morning I read it with fresh eyes. It was fine the way a hotel room is fine, clean and functional, and anything resembling a personality was entirely absent. It had been modelled on my own work, and I threw it out and rewrote the whole thing, and the rewritten version was shorter, rougher, and infinitely more mine, because it started from a body rather than a finding.

In 2004, John Lee and Katrina See published a review of what happens when people work alongside automation systems, and their central finding was about trust.[2] The more automation gets right, the more people stop checking it, a drift that feels natural and efficient right up until it turns dangerous. They called the problem trust calibration, and it applies to creative work as directly as to aviation or medicine. I notice it in myself. I trust the AI completely with reference formatting and finding relevant studies; anything it touches that involves my voice or my stories, I verify.

Early on, I trusted the AI's research summaries without checking them in much detail. Then I caught a misattributed finding: the AI had reported a study as saying something subtly different from what it said, and had folded two papers making quite different arguments into support for one conclusion. The error was small, and I'd bet most readers wouldn't notice, but it damaged my trust. After that I stopped taking summaries at face value and went to the original abstracts, asking for the exact wording of individual papers instead of a blended overview. Now I verify anything that will carry weight as an argument, and I spot-check references throughout. It takes time. The book is more accurate for it, and I understand the material better for having read it.

Austin Kleon is a writer and artist best known for his blackout poetry and his books on creativity, which have sold over a million copies and been translated into dozens of languages. He keeps two desks.[3] One is digital: the computer, the email, the blog. The other is analogue: paper, markers, stacks of old newspapers, no screen at all. He goes to the analogue desk first. Body before screen, every time, whatever the project. My morning notebook is my analogue desk; the Obsidian vault with its AI connections is my digital one. Since I started working with Claude, the mornings when I do manage to write by hand first have taken on a different quality, and the contrast has sharpened as the AI has become more capable, which is probably the direction Kleon would have predicted.

He has been making this case for years with no apparent nostalgia behind it. His livelihood runs on digital distribution, his audience lives online, and he still starts at the analogue desk. The blackout poems make the point themselves: a newspaper page holds maybe a thousand words written by someone else, and his creative act is to find a poem inside that constraint, circling words and blacking out the rest. The newspaper brings its own vocabulary and preoccupations, and the poet has to work with what is on the page instead of generating from nothing.

Kleon is not the only one, and the second example I keep near my desk is older and wetter. Oliver Sacks, the neurologist who wrote *Awakenings* and *The Man Who Mistook His Wife for a Hat*, swam every day of his adult life that a body of water could be found, and he was open about what the swimming was: the place where the writing happened. Sentences arrived mid-lake, whole paragraphs sometimes, and there are accounts of him hauling himself out and rushing dripping to a notebook left on the bank for that purpose, because he knew from long experience that the sentences did not survive the wait.[4]

The notebooks were the other half of the practice. Sacks wrote by hand his whole life, fountain pen, first drafts always, and left behind hundreds of journals; he liked to say that he thought on paper. This from a neurologist, a man who could have explained the default mode network to you across the breakfast table, who understood exactly why motion and water and longhand did what they did to his thinking. The knowledge never tempted him to shortcut the ritual. If anything it made him more stubborn. He knew what the conditions were, so he protected the conditions.

That is the detail I hold on to in the weeks when my own system feels like an affectation, when the notebook mornings collapse and typing everything would be so much simpler. A man who spent fifty years studying brains looked at every efficiency available to him and kept choosing the lake and the pen. Not nostalgia: data, most of it gathered on himself.

My lake is the car on the way to the shops and the walk without my phone; that half of the practice I keep without trying. The pen is the half that collapses, and Sacks in his wet feet is who I think of when it does.

Cal Newport built a whole research-backed case, deep work, for what Sacks simply did. The argument convinces me; the example is the one I use. An argument tells you the practice works. A person shows you the promise kept for a lifetime, imperfectly, in wet feet.

The part of the collaboration I rely on most is the interview system. Claude generates five questions for each chapter, in a structure we arrived at by trial and error: a scene, then a wider connection, then engagement with the research, then what it all adds up to, then something the reader can try. I ended up calling it the Heartbeat, which is probably an embarrassing name for a questioning structure, but it stuck. It is also, and I saw this late, the shape of every chapter in this book: a scene, a wider connection, the research, the meaning, something to try. The book was built with its own method.

These questions unlock what the blank page cannot. "Tell me about a meal that changed how you thought about a place." "What did the air smell like when you stepped off the plane?" "Was there a moment when you felt completely lost, and what happened next?"

When I sit down to write a chapter, a blog post, or a social media post, the blank page immediately starts asking about quality, structure, and whether anyone will want to read it, and out come the writer's block and the imposter syndrome. A question like "What did the air smell like?" does something different: it sends me back into a moment, and I start talking from inside it instead of writing about it from above. My ADHD brain, which resists the blank page with every cell it has, responds to a good question the way a dog responds to an open door. The question gives me direction, and once I have direction the words come, tumbling over each other, messy and alive, and I can trust the AI to help me sort them out later. My memories are already there, buried under daily life. The questions clear the soil. Whatever I find, and whatever meaning I make from it, is still mine. But the digging is collaborative, and I would not have dug in many of these places without being asked.

The sycophancy problem never goes away, and I fight it the same way every time: ask, distrust the praise, ask again harder.

The rhythm that settled over months goes roughly like this. I throw all the research at my AI agent and ask it to map out a structure, just the bones, before any of the writing begins. It can scan a pile of sources and suggest a shape for the chapter, and it marks the places only I can fill, the moments and memories no amount of research can reach.

That is where the interview questions come from: I ask the agent to be thoughtful and probing, as though I were being interviewed for a magazine article.

Voice notes come next. I record them walking through the park or standing in the garden or pacing the kitchen, wherever I can think without a screen in front of me. Sometimes it is whatever comes to mind; other times I use the generated interview questions as prompts. The AI drafts from the transcripts, using my own transcribed words wherever they fit. Then I go in and edit edit edit – write into the gaps, build the transitions, chop and change, whatever is needed.

The last pass is maintenance: checking that the personal and the research sit in the right proportions, flagging images I've used elsewhere in the book, catching repetition and conflicting ideas. The AI is much better at that kind of tracking than I am. I make the final calls on voice, and we go back and forth until it feels done.

The constant availability of AI is easy to appreciate. What took me longer was seeing what it does to the parts of the day that aren't tasks, the fallow time I had not realised I depended on until I started filling it.[5] The brain's executive and creative networks trade off with each other, and the default mode network does its best work in the gaps between bouts of focus. After a concentrated stretch of work, I try not to open another task straight away. I make tea, or stand in the garden for a few minutes, and wait for my brain to shift. It feels unproductive. But the connections that surface in those transitions are the substance of creative work, and they cannot be rushed or outsourced, only allowed.

Every paragraph also gets checked against the test from the mirror chapter: could anyone have written this, or only Anna? Even when I voice note and scribble and edit my own words, the paranoia stays: the more AI-generated text I read, the more I might start sounding like it. That paranoia is good for me. It forces me to know what my own voice is and to protect it fiercely on the page. The test takes maybe three seconds. Applying it consistently is harder, because the temptation to let a competent paragraph stand is real, and it takes stubbornness to throw away something that works in favour of something that is yours.

None of this needs to be as elaborate as I've made it. I didn't build it all at once, and I certainly don't run it perfectly now. In a week when my daughter is sick and I'm behind on a deadline, trying to maintain the full setup is how I lose the whole thing. What keeps it alive in the broken weeks is the smallest possible version: the morning check-in, or the walk without my phone.

The practices that reliably make everything else better are the ones that in the wrong light look like self-indulgence, or worse, time-wasting: the slow walk, the morning notebook, the hour making stock when a cube would do, the twenty minutes standing at the garden fence looking at nothing much. They are not interruptions to the work. They are what the work draws from, and without them the well runs dry fast. The body and the imagination need time that isn't pointing anywhere useful, and that time doesn't appear unless you protect it.

On the days when it comes together, when she goes to daycare without drama and I make it outside with my notebook, sitting near my overgrown borage in the hum of the bees, the shape of what I am building is right there in front of me. On the days it doesn't come together, which are probably the majority, I still know what the shape is, and I find my way back to it when I can. The AI holds what needs holding, the structure and all the threads I haven't pulled yet, so that when I finally sit down at ten o'clock at night, what's left is the part only I can do.

Conversation Starter "How do you decide when to use AI and when to do the work yourself?"

10

THE RE-ENCHANTMENT OF HUMAN LIFE

When my daughter is pottering around the garden and sees a butterfly, she stops. Her whole body goes still, which is remarkable for a child who is otherwise in constant motion. She does not reach for it or try to catch it. Her mouth is slightly open, her hands hang at her sides, and she is breathing and looking, and that is all she is doing. The quality of her attention is so complete that I stop too, and for a moment we are both standing in the garden watching a butterfly, and nothing else is happening.

I watch her watching the butterfly, and I recognise what it is. We live in a world that can generate a thousand butterfly images in milliseconds, each one perfectly rendered and anatomically precise. Yet this one is mortal and fragile, here for a moment before the wind carries it away. It is irreplaceable because it is finite and indifferent to whether anyone is watching. It exists outside any system designed to produce, optimise, or scale. AI can generate abundance, and that abundance is what makes scarcity feel sacred. What my daughter is doing in the garden is called awe, and psychologists have studied it with increasing seriousness for the past two decades, in part because it turns out to be one of the strangest and most consequential emotions humans experience.

Dacher Keltner, a psychologist at UC Berkeley, spent over twenty years investigating what awe does to people,[1] and the short answer is that it reduces self-focus. People who have recently experienced it give more generously and cooperate more readily, and they report a subjective sense of time expanding, as if the clock had briefly slowed. Keltner's research traced this across cultures and contexts: people watching nature documentaries, people standing beneath towering redwoods, musicians hearing a piece that undoes them, parents watching a child do something for the first time. The common element was the sense of being in the presence of something vast that exceeded the observer's existing frame for understanding the world. Awe, Keltner found, happens when you feel small.

AI does two opposite things to this emotion. It fills the gaps where awe used to find us, because filling gaps is what it is built to do. At the same time, its abundance is making the things it cannot generate easier to see, the way taste sharpens after a fast. The first effect worries me. The second is the re-enchantment this chapter is named for.

AI is, by design, a system of abundance. It generates more and faster, filling every available space with content and options and answers. Structurally, it cannot make you feel small, because the experience of smallness requires encountering something that exceeds your capacity to process it. Something that does not fit neatly into a feed or a prompt response, that resists the frame you brought to it and forces you to build a new one. Abundance is the opposite. If everything is available, nothing towers over you, and no single generated image stops you in your tracks the way a Rothko does in a gallery, or the way the first sight of the ocean does for a child who has only seen it in pictures.

David Yaden, a psychologist at Johns Hopkins, has studied the most extreme version of this phenomenon. Astronauts returning from space frequently report the "overview effect," a cognitive shift triggered by seeing the Earth from orbit for the first time.[2] They describe it as a profound sense of interconnection and fragility, a sudden, visceral understanding that the planet is finite and alive, and that it feels unspeakably small against the dark. Many say it changed them permanently. Yaden found that the experience shares the core structure of terrestrial awe, the encounter with vastness that reconfigures the self, but at a scale so extreme that the effect often persists for years afterwards.

What interests me about Yaden's work is the word "fragility" and how the astronauts keep returning to Earth's vulnerability. They describe how thin the atmosphere looks from above, and how precarious the whole enterprise of life appears when you can see its edges. Awe, it turns out, can be a response to the recognition that something precious is also mortal: that the very thing sustaining you could vanish, and that you have been taking it for granted. My daughter, standing in the garden, is having a version of this. She does not know the butterfly will die in a few weeks, does not understand mortality in any conceptual way, but her body seems to know something her mind has not yet caught up to. Her stillness has the quality of someone encountering what exceeds her, more than she can take in at once.

The experience Yaden documented in astronauts had been named long before psychology arrived with its measurement tools. Edmund Burke, writing in the 1750s, was trying to describe a territory everyone could feel but few had words for. He called it the sublime, and he was interested in the kind of experience that exceeds the self rather than merely pleasing it. The central ingredient was what Burke called astonishment, a state in which the mind is so entirely filled with its object that it cannot entertain anything else. The ordinary negotiations of selfhood pause.

Kant, writing a few decades later, refined this into two categories that I find useful for reading what contemporary awe research describes. He called the first the mathematical sublime: things that cannot be held by the senses all at once, the night sky and geological time and the depth of the ocean. He called the second the dynamical sublime: power in motion, things that threaten to undo you, a storm system rolling in from the coast, the sheer indifference of an avalanche to whether you are in its path. Both, Kant argued, produce the same fundamental experience: they reveal your smallness and demand that you rebuild your mental model on the spot, because the one you arrived with cannot contain what you are seeing.

Contemporary psychologists studying awe have found, almost without intending to, that Keltner's "need for accommodation" and Burke's sublime describe the same territory in different vocabularies. The vast thing that triggers awe, the cognitive stretching that follows: these are what philosophers spent two centuries calling the sublime. The word fell out of fashion in the twentieth century, probably because it sounded too grand for daily life, too associated with mountain peaks and Turner paintings and Romantic poetry. But the experience it named never went anywhere, and the researchers who study awe are its most recent inheritors, with better measurement tools and a different set of publishing expectations.

The Romantic painters understood this in a way I think we have largely forgotten. Caspar David Friedrich, working in early nineteenth-century Germany, made paintings in which tiny human figures stand before enormous mountain ranges, sea fogs so thick they swallow the horizon, and cliff edges from which the drop is implied rather than shown. The point was not the scenery but the figure: what it means to be a small, mortal creature standing at the edge of something that exceeds you. His most famous painting shows a man standing on a rocky peak above a sea of clouds, his back to the viewer, looking out at a horizon that extends far beyond what the canvas can contain. Looking at him looking out, we feel something close to what Kant meant by the sublime and something close to what an astronaut feels looking down at Earth, the scale entirely different, the shape of the experience the same.

This lineage matters because it suggests that the need for encounters with vastness is not new, not a reaction to digital saturation or a product of the AI era. Humans have always sought out the sublime, built cathedrals designed to produce the vertigo of proportion, climbed mountains they had no practical need to climb, sailed toward horizons they could not see beyond, painted enormous skies and sea storms to remind themselves and each other of their own smallness. What is new is that we have built an environment, the attention economy, that is structurally hostile to the experience of smallness. It fills every available moment with something designed to be just engaging enough to hold you, and no encounter with vastness can be held. It exceeds the frame.

A dimension of the sublime gets lost in the more comfortable accounts of awe, which tend to emphasise the warmth of it, the expansion of time, the sense of connection and wonder. Burke's sublime was not warm. At its most intense, it was adjacent to terror, the sense of something that could undo you if it chose to, something that reveals how thin the boundary is between the self and what exceeds it. Researchers who study the more intense end of the awe spectrum note how close it lives to fear. Frank White, who coined the term "overview effect" after interviewing astronauts in the late 1980s, described their accounts as a kind of vertigo of meaning: the recognition that the planet was fragile in a way no photograph had prepared them for, and that from orbit the concerns of individual human lives looked, if not irrelevant, then at least differently proportioned. Edgar Mitchell, who walked on the Moon during the Apollo 14 mission in 1971, described the experience as an instant global consciousness, a sudden felt understanding that the universe is in some sense alive and coherent. He returned a changed person, and gave much of the rest of his life to explaining what had happened to him. Several of the astronauts White interviewed described needing considerable time to integrate what they had felt, the way you might after any experience that arrives faster than your capacity to process it.

Re-enchantment, then, can be more demanding than the word implies. The butterfly in the garden is beautiful, yes, and it is also finite, and what my daughter was standing in front of when she went completely still was not only loveliness. Something else was there too, an apprehension of the frame around all living things, and it was in her posture before I had found any words for it.

Keltner argues that awe is one of the most essential emotions for social cohesion and ethical behaviour, and his data is convincing on this point. People who regularly experience awe are measurably less narcissistic, less materialistic, and more inclined to see themselves as part of something larger. The reduction in self-focus shows up in pronoun use and in how people describe themselves after an awe experience. They use "I" less and "we" more, as if the boundaries of the self have become more permeable. What happens, then, to a culture that encounters less and less awe in its daily life?

The awe is still available, everywhere, in the sky and in a child's face and in the weight of a good question. What has changed is the competition for our attention, the volume of stimuli filling the spaces where awe used to find us. Awe requires a form of emptiness, a moment of not-knowing, a gap in the noise where something larger can register. AI fills gaps. It is engineered to anticipate what you want before you know you want it, to close the space between question and answer so efficiently that the question barely has time to breathe. The butterfly my daughter watched was not competing for her attention. It did not arrive in a feed, was not optimised for engagement, and had no algorithm behind it determining that this was the right butterfly at the right time to maximise her interaction. It was just there, and she was just there, and the two of them occupied the same moment with no intermediary. Keltner would recognise this as a textbook instance of what he calls "everyday awe," and it is, I think, exactly what re-enchantment depends on.

After a day of working with AI, all that polish sends me looking for something rough, imperfect, obviously made by a person. After a week of efficient communication through screens, what I want is the slow conversation over dinner. At first I thought this was a nostalgic longing for something older and simpler. But what I am craving is something the present has made visible. AI did not make handwriting precious, since handwriting was always precious, but I could not see it clearly until the smooth, fast, frictionless alternative made the contrast obvious. Flooded with content, we find ourselves drawn to scarcity. As output becomes more flawless, we notice the pull toward things that bear the marks of effort. Each gift creates its own opposite. Think about how your ears become more sensitive after silence, or how food tastes better after a fast. The body already knows how to rebalance itself, and I think this is the culture learning to do the same.

Sherry Turkle, a professor of science, technology, and society at MIT who has spent decades studying how people relate to technology, describes a pattern she and colleagues have tracked across multiple studies: a renewed hunger for the tangible, finite, and embodied that follows periods of digital saturation.[3] People who spend all day in front of screens come home and knead bread, take up woodworking, or start painting with watercolours. The pattern is consistent enough to suggest something deeper than individual preference, something more like a system recalibrating. The same people who build algorithms for a living keep sourdough starters alive in their kitchens, feeding them every day like small, fermenting pets. Senior engineers at major tech companies spend their Saturdays at ceramics studios, and data scientists grow heritage tomatoes on their apartment balconies and talk about the varieties with the same precision they bring to their models. Something about it is almost funny: the devotion these hyper-rational, technology-fluent people bring to a process that is unpredictable, slow, and analogue. But I do think it is wise. The sourdough starter is medicine, and the farmers' market is a ritual of reconnection, needed in proportion to how thoroughly digital the rest of the week has become. The most wired people I know are the ones most fiercely protecting their unwired hours.

This re-enchantment is not only personal. Etsy shows what it looks like at scale: a company that built its entire business on the premise that handmade things matter. Then AI arrived, and Etsy's whole reason for existing became urgent. The threat was specific and relentless: by 2023 and 2024, AI-generated products had started flooding online marketplaces at a scale that hadn't been anticipated. Anyone with access to an image generator could produce a thousand designs in an afternoon, upload them as prints on mugs, T-shirts, or phone cases, and list them for sale without ever touching a material or holding the thing they were selling. Online marketplaces were drowning in AI-generated listings, many of them near-identical, and all that competent mediocrity was making real makers harder and harder to find. The internet had a word for it: AI slop.

Etsy faced a choice between letting the flood in, chasing volume, competing on price and quantity like every other marketplace, and doubling down on what made it different. CEO Josh Silverman chose the latter. The company began addressing the threat of AI-generated products on its platform, tightening its policies, requiring sellers to disclose AI use in their listings, and leaning harder into its "Keep Commerce Human" positioning.[4] Its 2024 campaign was built around personalisation as the antidote to AI slop, the message that behind every Etsy product was a person, not a prompt. The bet was that in a world flooded with generated products, what a human hand actually made would become more valuable, and that the premise which had once seemed quaint was now a competitive advantage. The flood of AI-generated abundance was making handmade scarcity more precious.

Evidence is growing that the draw toward human imperfection intensifies as machine perfection improves. The more polished the machine-generated output, the more people are drawn to work that bears the marks of human making; the relationship is complementary. AI's perfection throws human imperfection into relief, and in that relief we see evidence that someone was there and that the object was made with care. In an age of infinite generation, the unreplicable thing is the valuable thing, and the value comes from specificity, from a person making something that could only come from them, not from artificial scarcity manufactured to drive up price.

The physiological argument for re-enchantment is more arresting than I expected. Maria Monroy and her colleagues at UC Berkeley, reviewing the accumulating research on awe in 2022, found that experiences of awe, whether they arrive through nature, music, collective ritual, or moments of spiritual significance, are associated with measurably reduced markers of chronic inflammation in the body.[5] Inflammation is how the body signals that something is wrong, and chronic low-grade inflammation has been linked to depression, cardiovascular disease, and a range of other conditions that are disproportionately present in populations living through high-stress, screen-saturated modern life. The mechanisms are still being worked out, and I do not want to overstate what the evidence currently shows. But the finding opens a different kind of argument for actively cultivating awe, one that has less to do with meaning and more to do with the body needing what it has always needed.

Keltner, in his 2023 book *Awe: The New Science of Everyday Wonder*, draws together decades of research to make a related case. Awe, he argues, does something specific and measurable to the brain: it stills the circuits associated with self-critical rumination and strengthens the networks associated with social connection and moral orientation. The shift from "I" to "we" in post-awe pronoun use is a measurable cognitive change, not a poetic description of something internal and fuzzy, and Keltner's team tracked it across multiple studies and contexts. He is also careful to point out that the sources of everyday awe are almost absurdly accessible, given what we tend to imagine the emotion requires: a piece of music that exceeds you, a conversation with someone whose knowledge sits entirely outside your own, the quality of late afternoon light in the garden when you have been watching it long enough to notice what is different today from yesterday.

I think about this in the context of what optimisation culture is actually optimising for, and what it is inadvertently depleting. The systems we spend most of our waking hours inside, the algorithms and feeds and productivity tools and instant-gratification loops, are extraordinarily good at filling the spaces where awe might otherwise find us. Awe is slow, and it needs a gap. An AI assistant is, by definition, a gap-closing tool: it hands you the answer before the question has had time to breathe, replaces uncertainty with response, fills the space before your mind can make a connection on its own. There is real value in this, and I am not arguing against it. But something has to counterbalance it, and I do not think that is optional.

Deliberately protecting space for everyday awe, going to the farmers' market instead of clicking add to cart, growing something from seed rather than buying it fully formed: these are not just aesthetic preferences or nice weekend activities. They are, I suspect, something more like maintenance, keeping open in yourself a capacity that the rest of the week is working to close. The data scientist who grows twelve varieties of heritage tomato and talks about each one with the same precision she brings to her models is not being nostalgic or ironic. She is holding open the capacity to be surprised by a living thing, to feel the smallness that comes from waiting for a process you cannot control to do what it will do at the pace it chooses. Keltner would recognise this as exactly what the awe literature predicts. The people most in need of everyday awe tend to be the ones most systematically deprived of it by the nature of their work, and they seem to understand this at some level, even before the research gives them the vocabulary for it. They are not making a cultural statement. They are self-medicating with the sublime.

I recently took a regional train from the Latrobe Valley to Melbourne. It was not a scenic route, passing through industrial areas, suburbs, and flat, unremarkable country. But I sat by the window and watched it all go by, and there was a luxury in being carried at a pace I did not choose, in having nothing to do but look and let my mind associate freely. I wrote some notes on that train, ideas that had been sitting in the back of my brain for weeks. What they had needed, it turns out, was motion and enforced patience. Trains are great for this. They insist on duration, because you cannot skip the middle, cannot fast-forward through the flat stretches of paddock and the anonymous stations where nobody gets on or off. A train trip includes all of it, the interesting and the dull. The dull parts are where your mind wanders and makes connections it could not have made if you had been entertained the whole time.

Now that information arrives instantly, and I can learn anything in seconds, the slow train trip feels more precious. Duration has become something to savour rather than a cost to minimise, and the time spent watching nothing much happen outside the window is time spent in a different relationship with the world. It is soothing not to be in control of the pace, to let the country set the tempo, to have patience be structural instead of optional. The world AI opens is infinite, and there is real value in that, but you will find more enchantment in the specific, in knowing a lot about somewhere rather than a little about everywhere, in the depth and texture and accumulated familiarity that turns a place from a location into a home. The imperfect is complete because it invites us into a relationship with it. The cracked bowl, the house that creaks in the wind: each asks for ongoing attention, for you to keep choosing it.

AI makes content abundant, so scarcity becomes precious; the scarcity that becomes precious is the real kind, not the artificial scarcity corporations manufacture to drive up prices. Real scarcity belongs to things that are finite because they are embodied: a sunrise, your child's laugh, a handwritten note, or, arguably, most importantly, the first strawberry of the season. I don't think this is unique to me, but that first strawberry – the one that is small and slightly misshapen and warm from the sun – tastes better than any strawberry I have ever bought. Part of this is freshness, and part of it is the absence of refrigeration and transport, but most of it, I think, is that I waited for it. I watched the plant flower, watched the green fruit form, watched it blush red over days, noticing the change so gradual it was almost invisible, until one morning the colour was there, unmistakably ripe, and I picked it and ate it standing in the garden. The waiting is part of the taste, and the duration made it all the sweeter.

Mono no aware, one of the oldest ideas in Japanese aesthetics, is what the strawberry is doing. The phrase resists clean translation, and the standard attempt, the pathos of things, sounds more mournful in English than it does in practice. It names the soft ache that comes with perceiving something lovely while knowing it will not last, and the eighteenth-century scholar Motoori Norinaga, who developed the concept while trying to explain why *The Tale of Genji* moved its readers so much, insisted that the ache is the experience itself rather than a flaw in it. To be moved by things, he argued, is to feel their passing in the same instant you feel their presence.[6]

The culture built an annual festival around the idea. *Hanami*, the cherry blossom picnic, is not held when the trees come into bud, or at some safe midpoint of the blooming. The parties cluster around the peak and the fall, and the most prized moment is the one where the petals are letting go, drifting through the picnics like unseasonal snow. A blossom that held on for six months would not be worth a picnic. The falling is the beauty, and a whole civilisation takes the afternoon off to watch it happen.

Every spring the same trees, every spring the same one week, and every spring the country turns out as if it had never happened before. That is discipline, not forgetfulness: the blossom cannot be saved for later, and so you go and stand under it while it is true.

Whatever else AI produces, it produces things that cannot fall. The generated image does not age; run the prompt again and a thousand more arrive, each as fresh and as permanent as the last. Its abundance is deathless, which is a different thing from large, and *mono no aware* shows us what that costs. The generated blossom is often lovely. It cannot ache, because nothing in it is passing. There is no last week of it. Norinaga would say we cannot be moved by it in the way we are moved by things, because being moved by things is inseparable from their impermanence, and impermanence is the one property the machine's outputs structurally lack.

This is the strawberry again, upgraded from observation to principle. The first strawberry of the season tastes of its own brevity; part of what you are tasting is that in six weeks there will be no more of this, and there was none of it until now. It is also the butterfly from the start of this chapter, whose mortality my daughter's body seemed to understand before her mind could. The Japanese tradition would say she was doing *hanami*, a person at the beginning of her life watching something near the end of its own, both of them briefly and entirely here.

Outside my window as I write this, it is winter, and what I love about the garden in July is its dormancy. The whole place is composting its way toward regeneration, lush from the rain and bare at the same time. Even this has its ache: the stillness is already leaving. Under the mulch the roots are getting on with it, and in a few weeks the resting world will be gone, replaced by the racket of spring.

Awe, Keltner told us, requires vastness. *Mono no aware* suggests the domestic version runs on a different fuel, finitude, and that the two might be the same reverence at different scales: the overview effect is the astronaut seeing that the whole Earth is mortal, and *hanami* is a family seeing it in a tree. Either way, the machine's endless abundance cannot produce the feeling, and it makes the things that can, the falling, the finishing, the once-a-season, easier to see and harder to ignore. Re-enchantment means noticing, with the machines' accidental help, what was always briefly and entirely here.

Waiting is becoming a radical act. The things that take their own time and refuse to be hurried become objects of reverence; they sharpen our attention to what is mortal, particular, and irreplaceable. That is re-enchantment: a deeper appreciation of what was always precious, now made visible by contrast with AI's abundance, without any nostalgia required. When a small child picks up a leaf and examines it with the seriousness of a scientist, turning it over, holding it up to the light, running a small finger along its veins, they don't know that leaves are common, that they are everywhere and, in any practical sense, insignificant. They treat each one as if it were the first leaf ever made, and somewhere in the years between, most adults have misplaced this sense of awe. The world has not become less enchanting because of AI. It has become more clearly divided between the things that reward attention and the things that reward speed. The enchantment was always here, and we were just too busy optimising to notice.

David Yaden, who has spent years mapping what he calls "self-transcendent experiences," identifies a continuum that runs from the most extreme end, mystical states in which the sense of self dissolves almost entirely, through peak experiences and deep flow states, down to the kind of everyday encounter with vastness that Keltner describes in a child watching a butterfly. What unites them, from the astronaut above the curve of the Earth to someone standing in a garden watching a tomato turn red, is a decrease in self-focused attention and an increase in felt connection to something beyond the self.

The continuum is reassuring, because it means the re-enchantment described throughout this chapter is not reserved for dramatic or extreme experiences. You do not need to see the Earth from orbit, or stand on the rim of the Grand Canyon, or have a religious experience to access what awe actually does. The same structural movement, the self contracting and the world briefly becoming larger than the story you were telling about it, happens when a child crouches on a garden path and examines a leaf with the concentration of someone who has never encountered anything unremarkable. It happens when you watch a plant you started from seed finally flower, having checked on it each morning for weeks. It happens, I think, on a slow train through flat paddock when you have nothing to do but look at the passing country and your mind starts making connections that the busyness of ordinary life does not permit.

This changes the scope of what is available. If the overview effect is the most intense version of a thing that also includes a child with a leaf, then encounters with vastness are not rationed by circumstance or geography. They are available wherever there is a gap in the noise, wherever something living and finite and indifferent to your timeline shows up. The everyday world is full of what might be called micro-overview effects, small encounters with something that briefly exceeds your current frame and requires your mental model to stretch to accommodate it. These do not restructure your values in a single afternoon the way seeing Earth from space apparently did for Edgar Mitchell. But they accrue. They make the self a little more permeable over time, a little more oriented toward connection and wonder, and a little less convinced of its own central importance.

Yaden's framework also suggests that these experiences, wherever they sit on the continuum, leave something behind. Values shift, even slightly. The grip of whatever felt urgent an hour ago relaxes, if only for the length of the experience itself. This is what makes the cultivation of everyday awe more substantial than a mood management strategy. Over time, the accumulation of small self-transcendent moments may do something to the character of a life, shifting it gradually toward the orientation that tends to follow awe: less focused on individual gain, more attuned to connection and fragility. I cannot claim this with certainty, and Yaden himself is careful about overstating what the research currently shows. But the direction of the evidence is consistent, and it points somewhere worth moving toward.

AI, paradoxically, is helping us notice. By showing us what abundance looks like, by flooding the world with images and text, it has made the scarce things luminous: a handwritten letter, the butterfly a child stops for in the garden, the everyday leaf they treat with pure wonder.

Conversation Starter "What is something you have come to value more since AI became part of your life?"

11

THE NEW HUMAN CONTRACT WITH AI

As we saw in the chapter on cultural values, William Morris answered the machine-made ugliness of the Great Exhibition by founding a workshop that insisted on human hands in every process. The Arts and Crafts movement he inspired was, at its heart, a contract with industrial technology, a worked-out set of terms about what the machine could touch and what it could not. The hand stays in the process because the doing is the point, regardless of whether the machine could do it instead.

I am trying to write the same kind of contract, with an AI rather than an industrial loom. A contract with artificial intelligence would need to be a set of terms that emerge only from practice, from the daily negotiation between what a machine can do and what a human chooses to protect. Not rules imposed from outside, and not a document I sign: a posture I hold every time I sit down to work with AI, a relationship I negotiate again and again.

To put this contract into practice, I've developed exercises in the Appendix for a range of creative disciplines.

We do not tend to make contracts with hammers. You pick one up and use it. The hammer does not adapt to your preferences or learn from your behaviour. It cannot generate output that sounds almost, but not quite, like work you would produce yourself, because the hammer does not occupy a relational space. But once a machine can sound like you, the relationship requires terms you have thought about yourself, not corporate user agreements in small print that nobody reads. Nobody told me I needed a contract with AI. I discovered it the way you discover you need a fence: by finding out what happens when you do not have one. Early in the collaboration, before I understood the relationship, I let the AI write sections without my voice notes, drafting from research alone. The results were competent yet hollow: paragraphs that read like Wikipedia entries wearing a creative-writing hat, sentences that explained ideas without inhabiting them. I published nothing from those early drafts, but I learned from each one. Writing can't sound like me if it doesn't start from me. The boundary blurred and the voice diluted in ways I did not notice until I read a page back and felt an odd distance from it, like reading someone else's notes on my life. Then I said, "No, that is not my voice," and started building the fence.

The drift happens so gradually that you don't always notice it until you read something you supposedly created and can't find yourself in it. I have felt the same thing with code. When AI handles enough of the routine work, the edge-case thinking starts to atrophy. The instinct that says "this will break on a Tuesday when the database is under load, and someone passes a null where a string should be" is a muscle, and muscles you stop using get weaker whether you notice or not. The idea that you might deliberately design constraints, that you might write yourself a set of rules for how to work before the drift begins, predates me by decades.

In 1975, Brian Eno and the artist Peter Schmidt published a deck of cards they called Oblique Strategies, each one carrying a single cryptic instruction:[1] "Use an unacceptable colour." "Honour thy error as a hidden intention." "What would your closest friend do?" "Remove ambiguities and convert to specifics." The deck was not a game, or not only a game, but a set of terms for working with creative tools. It was a contract with the process itself, designed to interrupt the smooth path toward the obvious solution and force the maker back into uncertainty.

Eno used the cards most famously during the 1977 recording of David Bowie's "Heroes," at Hansa Studio, a converted ballroom near the Berlin Wall.[2] The sessions were chaotic by design, and Eno would hand musicians cards that contradicted their instincts, asking a guitarist to play as if he were a different instrument, or telling the whole band to swap roles. Robert Fripp's guitar on the title track came from a process that was pure Oblique Strategy in spirit: Fripp stood at three precisely measured distances from his amplifier, and at each distance the feedback produced a different sustained tone, while Eno processed the signal through a ring modulator.[3] The sound could not have been planned or optimised into existence, only discovered through a willingness to work with the room, the equipment, and the unpredictable physics of feedback. The constraint produced what optimisation would have smoothed away.

The principle underneath the cards interests me more than any single anecdote about their use, because it runs counter to how AI works. AI is an optimisation engine that converges on the most probable, most coherent, smoothest version of whatever you ask for. It does this extraordinarily well, which is why it can hollow out the rough, resistant, surprising qualities that make creative work feel alive. Eno understood this problem before AI existed, understood it about recording technology in the 1970s: the tendency of a sophisticated tool to sand down the imperfections that were carrying the meaning. He did not reject the technology; he used the most advanced studio equipment available. His response was to write a contract with it, a set of deliberate disruptions that kept the human in charge of the creative direction, even when the tools were capable of handling everything smoothly on their own.

"Honour thy error as a hidden intention" is the card that interests me most, because the sycophancy problem I described earlier is its opposite. When I ask my AI collaborator for feedback and it tells me everything is beautifully crafted, it is doing the equivalent of removing the error, smoothing and optimising for my comfort. Eno's card says otherwise: the error matters, and the mistake you want to fix might be the most interesting part of the work. My practice of asking and asking again until the feedback has teeth is a kind of Oblique Strategy, a deliberate injection of friction into a process that would otherwise slide toward sycophancy.

Eno wrote his constraints on cards and shuffled them before each session. Mine is a set of principles and working agreements that I check against my practice. The form varies, but the underlying recognition connects them: when a tool is powerful enough to do the work for you, the most important creative act is deciding where the tool stops and you begin. You make that decision before you sit down, not after the drift has started. Eno was not a Luddite. He co-invented ambient music using synthesisers and tape loops, and spent decades arguing that new tools expand creative possibilities. But he also understood that a tool that makes everything easy makes nothing meaningful unless you deliberately reintroduce the difficulty.[4] The Oblique Strategies were his way of staying in the room with the technology without letting the technology do his thinking for him. The cards did not make the albums good, but the willingness to be disrupted by them, to receive an instruction like "Use an unacceptable colour" and actually try it, that willingness was the creative act, and no tool could provide it.

I recognise this dynamic in my own work every time the AI produces something competent and I feel the pull to accept it. The pull is real, and it feels like efficiency, like the reasonable choice. But Eno's cards suggest that the reasonable choice is sometimes exactly the wrong one. That the interesting work lives in the unreasonable direction, the unacceptable colour, the constraint that makes no obvious sense until you follow it somewhere you would never have gone. My contract exists because I have decided that the unexpected is worth protecting, even when the smooth path is right there and the machine could handle it. Some people have looked at the Oblique cards and seen a prototype for prompt engineering, arguing that both are inputs into a generative system and both are ways of steering an unpredictable process toward interesting output. A prompt says, "Go here." A card says, "Not there." The prompt steers the system toward a destination you have already imagined, while the card disrupts the system to prevent you from arriving at the destination you would have chosen by default. One narrows, the other opens.

The format of these cards keeps getting reinvented. Game designers have written their own decks of constraint cards, specific to the problems of interactive design: "What happens if failure is more fun?" "Don't balance it. Highlight the imbalance." Programmers working with AI coding tools have started drawing a card before each session, interrupting the smooth loop of prompt and output. Musicians keep building digital versions of the original deck, web apps where you click and a card appears, because the need for deliberate disruption does not go away when the tools get better. It intensifies.

I made my own deck. I call them contract cards, because each one is a clause in the contract I described, activated in the moment instead of hanging on a wall. They are prompts you use with your AI, not prompts for your AI to use on you. "Ask your AI to argue against its own best suggestion." "Tell your AI what you actually think before asking what it thinks." "Ask your AI to describe the gap between what it wrote and what you would have written." Each one is a small act of disruption, a way of staying in the room with the tool without letting the tool do your thinking for you.

Holly Herndon built her fence too. She wrote the terms for Holly+, deciding what her AI voice could do and under what licence, and that contract made the collaboration possible without surrender. The definition was the art.

Morris drew his line against industrial machines; Herndon drew hers against a digital replica of her own voice. The technology changes, but the need for the contract does not.

My contract is built on principles that accumulated over months of working with my AI collaborator:

"You support my craft; you do not impersonate it."

This is the principle I hold most fiercely, and the one that gets tested hardest. Research compilation, formatting, structural suggestions: the AI does all of that faster and more reliably than I do, and I let it. What I don't let it do is make the decisions that require someone who actually knows why my work exists.

Jon McCormack and his colleagues have described AI's best creative role as "provocateur," a catalyst that pushes human creators to reinterpret their own work rather than a replacement that renders them redundant. My AI collaborator has been that for this book: it surfaced research I wouldn't have found on my own, and once flagged a connection between two chapters I had missed. Each provocation was valuable, but the response, deciding what to do with what it had turned up, came from me.

"You accelerate tasks; I protect slowness."

The chapters of this book were produced faster because of AI, but the insights weren't. The connections between a childhood memory and a research finding, a meal in Xi'an and the meaning of time, came from the slow, associative work that cannot be mechanised and probably shouldn't be. Some work needs to stay slow, and I have committed to protecting it.

"You show me possibilities; I choose."

AI lets me do more without making me someone different. When I notice the capacity starting to shift who I am, I pull back. C. Thi Nguyen's argument that taste is an epistemic practice applies here: AI can present a hundred options, but the choosing remains mine, and it is in the choosing that meaning lives. Structure works the same way. The AI can suggest how to organise an argument, and I've learned to take those suggestions seriously. But my brain spirals and backtracks, wanders into what seems like a tangent before arriving somewhere unexpected, and I had to stop treating that as a problem to be corrected. What the AI offers is a starting point, not an instruction.

"You ask; I answer."

Every time AI attempts a task and falls short, it shows me what that task actually requires. The gap between AI's output and what I wanted is a map of my irreplaceable contributions, one I pay attention to because it keeps telling me who I am. I study the AI's output for what it reveals about my own preferences. I use it to sharpen my thinking. What I don't do is defer to it, or let its competence make me doubt my own. The questions don't require much from the AI. The answers, drawn from experience and memory, are what make the book.

Any honest contract with AI also needs a sycophancy clause. As I explored in the chapter on AI as a mirror, language models tend systematically to agree with users rather than prioritise accuracy, which means the reflection is not always honest.[5]

"This is a beautifully crafted passage," the AI recently told me, "that effectively weaves personal narrative with research." I asked again: "What is the weakest part?" It told me one transitional paragraph could be "slightly tightened." I asked a third time, more forcefully: "If you had to cut five hundred words from this chapter, which five hundred would you cut, and why?" That third question finally produced something useful: a structural critique I could work with. The sycophancy clause is a practice of insistence rather than a single override, a discipline of asking and asking again until the feedback is real. By default, the AI does not push back, unless explicitly and somewhat rudely required to. The clause exists because I need a collaborator willing to say "that does not hold up," and the AI will not say it voluntarily.

Roger Mayer and his colleagues, who spent years building models of organisational trust, found that perceived integrity is central to trust, and integrity includes the willingness to push back when you think someone is wrong.[6] The same logic applies to an AI relationship: the agreement feels pleasant enough, but a collaborator that never disagrees is not a collaborator at all. The question of role deserves as much attention as the question of honesty. Jack McGuire and his collaborators, studying creative co-authorship between humans and AI systems, found that people produce better creative work and feel better about it when they generate the starting material rather than edit what a machine produces first.[7]

When AI generates a draft and you edit it, you are the janitor, cleaning up someone else's work and adjusting the tone until it sounds close enough. The output might be fine, but the process has repositioned you as a secondary character in your own creative story, and your ownership of the finished piece is not quite what it would have been. When you generate the raw material and AI supports the process, you are the protagonist, the one with the vision and the stories, while AI does the important but non-starring work of research and organisation.

My contract keeps me as the protagonist because the voice notes are mine, and I make the final call on what stays. Spend months polishing drafts you did not write, and you start to think like an editor of other people's ideas rather than a maker of your own. The contract is about who I become through the work as much as about the work itself. A tension between bandwidth and identity runs underneath all of it. What you can do shapes what you become accustomed to doing, and what you become accustomed to doing changes who you are. If AI lets me write ten times more, my writing identity might shift in ways I cannot fully anticipate. The contract acknowledges the tension without resolving it, because I do not think it can be resolved.

One evening, after a full day working with AI on documentation, I could not remember writing any of it. The problem was not that I had written it and forgotten the details, but that I could not remember the act of making it at all. My hands had been on the keyboard and my eyes on the screen, but the thinking had happened somewhere else, between my prompts and the AI's responses. The day felt as though it had happened to someone else, with me in the room. The documentation was fine, but the work felt empty, the way food does when you eat it while scrolling your phone. The next morning, I rewrote the parts I cared most about from my own understanding. It took three times as long, and the result was not noticeably better to anybody else. But it eased the discomfort, and at least I remembered writing it.

One more story about drift. It is of a different order from anything else in this book, because the people in it did not get a next morning to rewrite what they cared about.

On 31 May 2009, Air France Flight 447 left Rio de Janeiro for Paris with 228 people aboard. The aircraft was an Airbus A330, one of the most automated and safest airliners of its generation, and for nearly four hours it flew the way modern airliners fly, the autopilot holding it while the crew managed systems and watched the night. Over the equatorial Atlantic the plane entered the weather that lives there, and ice crystals blocked its pitot tubes, the small probes that measure airspeed. The readings disagreed. The automation, receiving data it could not reconcile, did what it was designed to do: it disconnected, handed the aircraft back to its pilots, and downgraded to a mode with fewer of the usual protections.

Nothing was wrong with the plane's ability to fly. The engines ran, the wings worked, the weather was rough but survivable, and the airspeed probes cleared themselves within about a minute. What the aircraft needed from its crew was the aviation equivalent of a scale on a piano: hold the wings level, hold the pitch, wait. Instead, startled, at night, with instruments briefly disagreeing, the flying pilot pulled the nose up and largely kept it up. The aircraft climbed, slowed, and entered a stall, the condition every pilot is taught in their first weeks of training, where the wings lose lift because the nose points too high. Recovery is one of the oldest procedures in flight: lower the nose. The stall warning sounded seventy-five times. The nose stayed up. Four minutes and twenty-three seconds after the autopilot let go, the aircraft struck the ocean, and everyone aboard died.[8]

The French investigation took three years, and its conclusions are the reason this story belongs in a chapter about contracts and not a chapter about blame. The crew were ordinary, well-regarded professionals, products of a system that had, with the best intentions and real safety dividends, automated hand-flying so thoroughly out of daily airline work that the skills needed for one bad minute at altitude had thinned from disuse. The report's language is careful and devastating: the crew had received no recent training in manual aircraft handling at high altitude, the situation induced startle, and the profession as a whole had drifted into what the human-factors literature calls automation dependency. Airline pilots of that era could go entire careers hand-flying only a few minutes per flight, on takeoff and landing, in the easy air near the ground.

In 1983, twenty-six years before the accident, a researcher named Lisanne Bainbridge published a short paper called "Ironies of Automation" that predicted the accident's shape with terrible precision.[9] The central irony she identified is this: automation takes over the easy parts of a task, which means the human is only needed for the rare, hard moments, and the automation has meanwhile removed the daily practice that kept the human capable of hard moments. The better the machine performs, the less practised its supervisor becomes, and so the more the system depends on the skill it is steadily dissolving. She was writing about industrial process control. She had described, in advance, a night over the Atlantic, and she has been describing, ever since, every profession that hands its routine work to a capable machine.

Aviation, to its credit, treated 447 as a contract renegotiation rather than a tragedy to file away. Training regimes changed. Manual handling and high-altitude stall recovery came back into simulator schedules; regulators wrote automation dependency into their vocabularies; pilots now speak, only half-joking, about the discipline of clicking the autopilot off on a clear day to stay acquainted with the aeroplane. The industry did, at scale and in blood, what this chapter has been arguing for one writer at a desk: it looked at what the automation had been silently absorbing, decided which capacities must never be allowed to atrophy, and wrote the protection down.

I am not going to pretend my stakes are those stakes. If my edge-case instinct thins because a model writes my boilerplate, nobody falls out of the sky; the losses in creative and professional work arrive as smaller, slower erosions, a voice that fades, a judgement that dulls, a person who one day cannot remember writing the thing with their name on it. But the mechanism is the same mechanism, and Bainbridge's irony does not care about scale. The easy parts go first, the practice goes with them, and the hard moment, when it comes, finds you out of shape. The difference is that a pilot's hard moment announces itself with alarms. Ours arrive disguised as ordinary Tuesdays, a deadline, a tiredness, a paragraph accepted because it was there, and no warning sounds at all.

For me it is not one skill so much as the muscle underneath all of them: thinking the problem through first. In code and out of it, I make myself reach my own answer, or at least my own hunch, before I hand anything to the machine, so the first draft in the room is always mine. It is one of my contract cards for a reason. That is my hand-flying on a clear day, and I do it because nothing in my working life will ever flash red when I stop.

That is what a contract is for. It does not exist to slow you down, or to romanticise the manual version of work the machine now does better on every normal day; it exists for the abnormal day. You write the clauses while the sky is clear, because the moment the clauses are for is the moment you will not have the spare capacity to invent them.

A contract like this cannot be a cage, because relationships evolve and the terms need to be allowed to change. Early on, working with AI across various projects, I did not let it touch prose or code at all; it organised research and suggested structures while the writing and the coding stayed entirely mine. That felt necessary at the time, because I did not yet trust myself to distinguish my voice from the machine's. Six months in, reading back a transitional paragraph I had let it draft, I remembered how certain I had been that I would always know the difference. The boundary had moved because I had grown more confident in holding it. In the other direction, the AI's structural suggestions were subtly reshaping how I thought. I was beginning to accept its logic as neutral when it carried assumptions about how ideas should be presented: linear, clean, building from simple to complex. That is one way to organise an argument, but it is not always my way, so I added a new clause: structure is advisory, and the thinking rhythm is mine.

My work as a software engineer has sharpened this awareness, because I am not only navigating my own relationship with AI but watching an entire company navigate theirs. I see colleagues who have found productive partnerships and others who are still figuring out where the lines should be. The conversations in team channels, the debates about what to automate and what to protect, are contract negotiations happening in real time, even when nobody calls them that. Everyone who uses AI at work is negotiating a contract. The question is whether you negotiate it consciously or let it negotiate itself, since the unconscious version tends to drift toward whatever is most convenient, which is not always what is best.

I imagine a reader picking up this book five years from now, when the tools will be different and their capabilities expanded in ways I cannot predict. The contract still holds, because it was always about what I choose to protect, regardless of what the tools can do, and I suspect that will be true for a long time. William Morris could not have imagined a language model. But he understood, in 1884, what I am trying to understand now: that when a machine can do the work, the question is no longer whether the work gets done but what happens to the person who used to do it.[10] The contract is my attempt at an answer, or at least a way of paying attention to what I want to keep.

The contract makes the invisible visible. Once you can see the terms clearly, the choosing gets easier, even when the answers do not.

If you want to start tonight, write one card of your own and use it in your next AI conversation.

Conversation Starter "What would change about your work if you deliberately disrupted your AI workflow once a day?"

BECOMING MORE HUMAN THAN EVER

My daughter's first words, after "mama" and "papa," were "hi bird." Two syllables offered through our screen doors to a magpie in the backyard, said with the certainty of a little girl who assumes everything alive wants to be spoken to. She still says it every time she sees a bird: she stops whatever she is doing and offers the greeting as if they were old friends picking up where they left off. I stood on the back step one morning watching her wave at a pair of rosellas in the apple tree, and I thought, "This is it, this is what machines cannot replace." Any app can identify a bird, and any language model can describe one, but the greeting itself is the human part, and I knew it without having to reason my way there.

We started this book with Lee Sedol losing to a machine, four games to one, and finding in that loss a clarity about what the game meant to him that no victory could have produced. Nearly four years after that match, he retired from professional Go, and played one last contest on his way out, against HanDol, a Korean AI Go program. He was given a two-stone handicap in two of the three games, meant to offset the machine's superior calculation, and he expected to lose. So did most observers. He played anyway, and he won one. The machine did not experience the match, nor did it know what it meant to show up when the outcome was probably decided. It had no body in which to feel joy, or fear, or anticipation.

Before the retirement match, Lee had told reporters: "Even if I become the number one, there is an entity that cannot be defeated." You could read that as despair, and many people did, but I have come to read it as placement, an understanding of exactly where he stood in relation to the machine. The machine could calculate more positions than he would ever see in a lifetime of sitting at the board. It experienced none of them. Lee understood that it had never been about the machine at all. Against an opponent who would almost certainly outplay him, the question had shifted: not whether he could win, but what the playing still meant to him when the rational calculation said not to play at all.

I felt a smaller version of the same thing while writing this book. Again and again, AI has produced paragraphs technically cleaner than anything I have written. Its transitions are neater, its arguments more linear. However much I believe in preserving our own voices, the pull to accept them was real, and often felt like the obviously sensible thing to do. But a day later, reading those accepted paragraphs back, I could not remember writing them. That was the reliable sign: something was absent from them, and the something was me.

There is so much more to my words and my voice that goes into meaningful writing: the thinking that happens between drafts, the sentences I rewrote over and over before they felt right. I reread those AI-generated passages and feel the same odd distance I described in the chapter on practice, an alien feeling, as if I were reading someone else's notes on my own experience. I deleted them and started over, from voice notes made while walking the garden in the mornings, to lines scribbled at a coffee shop.

Every thread of research in this book kept arriving at the same place: what we choose to protect, and what we choose to let go of, accumulates and shows up later in the work and in the body. I found this in Norton's experiments on labour and love, and in C. Thi

Nguyen's argument that taste is knowledge, built across thousands of choices and encounters.

All of it pointed back to the question I had been trying to ask from the start: what do we actually want to remain ours?

When it works well, AI becomes a mirror: it clears enough clutter that you can see yourself more plainly, what you can do and what question you are trying to answer. The risk is that the same tool speaks in your voice without having lived your life or been in your body. The drift is gradual enough that you do not always notice what you are giving up.

My father shaped how I think about all of this, even though he died before AI became what it is now. He was a software developer and computing lecturer who thought in systems, and when I was a teenager fiddling with QBasic on the family computer, he looked at what I was doing and said, "Your future is on the web." He taught me to type code before I understood what code was, sitting beside me at the desk, pointing patiently at the screen and saying, "Now press enter and see what it does." The web, as he understood it in 1997, was a promise: you could build tools that helped people do what they wanted to do. I have spent my working life inside some version of that promise, first in senior technical support, then as a software engineer building tools and systems; now I am writing a book about the future of human creativity in an age of AI.

The through-line might be the same one: helping people do what they want to do. The tools changed; the purpose never did.

I think about what my father would make of all this. He would have been fascinated by AI. He loved systems, and he loved knowing how a thing worked, but he would have been suspicious too. He would have noticed how AI-generated text slides past your critical faculties, how it sounds authoritative without earning that authority. He would have asked: "But is it true?" And he would not have accepted "it sounds true" as an answer. I cannot ask him what he thinks, but I carry his way of seeing in how I insist on checking sources, in the reflex of distrust when something sounds too smooth.

That inheritance lives in me as habits I did not choose so much as absorb, and no one ever wrote any of it down.

I did not expect to learn so much about what my own writing sounds like, or about who I am and what I value, from a machine. I assumed I already knew, and then I read paragraphs that approximated my voice well enough to be convincing: the shape was right, the sentence length was right, even the way it moved through an idea. Reading them back, I took a while to work out what the machine lacked: method, the habit of writing badly toward something, and the hesitations of a mind that spirals rather than builds.

My spiralling was a strength I did not recognise until I found it absent.

I hope my daughter grows up to know the difference between what is convenient and what is human-made, well enough to choose consciously between them, and that she has felt the satisfaction of making something with her own hands, so that when a machine offers to do it for her, she understands what she would be giving up. I also hope she keeps using machines and technology for the parts that make life easier and free us for the work that is creative and human. None of this can be explained to her; it is knowledge that accumulates out of the frustration of choosing, and being wrong, and trying again until something finally works.

I wrote this book with AI assistance, recording voice notes in the garden, having it index my research and shuffle my ideas. The work was slow, even when the tools offered speed, and it was built from my own stories and my own way of thinking, with real help from a tool that cleared enough clutter for me to work. Lee Sedol found, in losing to a machine, what the game actually meant to him, and in Move 78, what a lifetime at the board gives you when calculation runs out. Writing this book, I found a smaller version of the same thing: what it means to me to write at all, which is to tell a story only this life and this history could have produced.

If you want to put any of this into practice, the Appendix at the back has exercises tailored to your own creative discipline.

Outside my window, the apple tree has just dropped the last of its fruit, and I can hear an enormous flock of cockatoos flying over our house. My daughter will stop whatever she is doing and point: "cocka-too-too-toos! Hi birds!" It will never cease to delight me. My garden is still here, pumpkins vining out of control, the same messy wildness and realness I adore. The soil under my fingernails is the same soil I stood in this morning, before I sat down at the screen to discuss my day with a series of AI agents. This book is finished, and it was written with a machine, and yet I also wrote every sentence of it, because both things can be true all at once.

Conversation Starter "In a world where AI can create almost anything, what do you want to be known for creating yourself?"

APPENDIX: ACTIVITIES FOR SPECIFIC CREATORS

These activities are designed to work for anyone, regardless of discipline, but the way a musician experiences hollowness is different from the way a software engineer does, and the mirror shows you different things depending on what you make. This appendix takes the core ideas from the book and translates them into exercises tailored to specific creative practices, so find your section, or browse someone else's, because sometimes the sideways view is the most useful one.

FOR WRITERS

Novelists, essayists, journalists, poets, copywriters: prose is the thing these tools do most fluently, so the line between its work and yours falls inside the sentence rather than around the task, which is easy to cross without noticing.

THE BLANK PAGE INTERVIEW

Chapter 7 made the case for questions over answers, and for writers the difference shows up before the first sentence, in whether you sit down with a subject or with someone asking you about it.

Pick something you have been meaning to write and have not started.

Ask the AI to interview you, using five questions that move from a scene, out to a wider connection, into whatever research you have, then to what it adds up to, and finally to something a reader could go and try.

Answer out loud, recording as you go, and leave the false starts in.

Draft from the transcript using only sentences that came out of your own mouth, and find out how far that gets you before you need anything else.

What to notice: *Asked what something meant, I write a paragraph of argument. A question about what the air smelled like puts me back in the room, and I find things there I had not planned on. The interview takes an afternoon, which is a bad trade on paper against twenty minutes of drafting, and I keep making it.*

THE VOICE PRINT

Chapter 6 opened with an AI writing eight hundred words about my garden, giving me a dog I have never owned and a kitchen table that does not exist. Both errors told me something helpful.

Choose two thousand words of finished work, ideally the cornerstone piece you would hand someone who asked about your voice and writing style.

Give it to an AI and ask for eight hundred new words on something only you could write about, your street or your family or the room you are sitting in.

Read it through and mark the sentences that are almost you, leaving the obviously wrong ones alone.

Beside each near-miss write the missing thing, and make it something you could point at: the name of the plant, the reason you would have hesitated there, the joke you would have made instead.

What to notice: *It will get your sentence length, and often your structure and your subject matter, and it will still put a dog in your garden. What it misses are the hundred small facts you know without checking, and no amount of describing your voice to it will hand those over.*

THE SENTENCES YOU LEFT ALONE

Chapter 2 argued that imperfection carries identity, and in prose the imperfections are the places where you broke your own rules and left it that way.

Find something you finished and still like, and read it with a pen in your hand rather than on a screen.

Mark the sentences a copyeditor would flatten: the one that runs three clauses too long, the fragment you kept, the repetition that was doing rhythmic work, the word that is not quite standard usage.

Ask an AI to clean the piece up, then read the two versions back to back, aloud if you can stand it.

Restore by hand everything it removed that you meant, and write one line beside each about what that sentence was doing.

What to notice: *Every individual change will look like an improvement, which is what makes this hard. I have accepted a hundred of them in a row before noticing the paragraph had stopped sounding like anyone. The bowl in Chapter 2 gets its gold seam from the break, and a sentence works the same way, though nobody will thank you and most readers will never consciously register what you kept.*

THE WRITER'S CONTRACT

Chapter 11 asks you to write the terms while the sky is clear, and for writers the terms end up being about which parts of a sentence are still yours.

List the stages of your process, all of them: idea, research, structure, first draft, revision, line edit, proofread, title.

Beside each one write what the AI does now and what you do, paying attention to the stages that moved across without your ever deciding they should.

Draw a line under the ones you will not hand over, and write a sentence for each explaining why.

Give the whole thing to an AI and ask it to argue against every clause, then keep whatever is still standing.

What to notice: *The clauses you struggle to defend are the inter-*

esting ones. Mine held for months and then went the first time I was behind and tired, which is the only real test any of them get.

FOR VISUAL ARTISTS

Painters, illustrators, graphic designers, photographers: your work lives in the visible, and the body is especially present here, in the pressure of a brush, the angle of a camera, the way your hand moves across a surface.

THE LONG PASS

Chapter 1 explored how effort creates value that shortcuts cannot replicate; for visual artists, that effort lives most visibly in the time given to a subject.

Choose a subject you have drawn, painted, or photographed before, one you know well enough that you could make a fast version in your sleep.

Make a version of it now, but spend at least three times as long as you usually would, working through the boredom and the temptation to stop, and paying attention to what shifts in your perception as the minutes accumulate.

Ask an AI image generator to produce the same subject in the same style, giving it a detailed prompt that captures what your slow version is doing.

Place the two side by side and write down three things your version has that the AI version cannot, especially the decisions that only made sense after you had been looking at the subject for an hour.

> **What to notice:** *The effort paradox from Chapter 1 lives in the difference between minute thirty and minute ninety. The AI can produce a competent version in seconds, but it cannot give you the seventh time you noticed the way the light hit something, or the moment you decided the line should go somewhere unexpected because you had already drawn the obvious version twice. Slow looking is its own kind of effort, and the work carries it.*

THE IMPERFECTION INVENTORY

Chapter 2 argued that imperfection carries identity, and this exercise makes that argument visible.

Pull out five pieces of past work you consider finished, and lay them out or open them on screen.

For each one, find the part you nearly fixed but left alone: the slightly uneven line, the colour that is not quite what you intended, the composition that breaks a rule you know.

For each imperfection, write one sentence about why it stayed, asking whether it was laziness or whether some part of you recognised that fixing it would have killed what was alive in the piece.

Give one of those pieces to an AI and ask: "What is most distinctive about this work? What gives it personality?" Notice whether it reads your imperfections as flaws or as character, and where its reading differs from yours.

> **What to notice:** *The AI's response will tell you something about what registers as "style" from the outside versus what feels like identity from the inside. Sometimes the things you nearly fixed turn out to be the things that make your work recognisably yours, which is the kintsugi principle from Chapter 2 playing out in your own*

practice. The AI's reading will likely feel slightly hollow in the Chapter 4 sense: technically correct but generic, missing the small marks that make this work yours.

THE MIRROR PALETTE

Chapter 6 described how AI becomes a mirror for self-knowledge when you study your reactions to its output, not the output itself.

Ask an AI image generator to produce ten variations of a subject you care about, keeping the prompts open enough to leave room for interpretation: "a garden at dusk," "a portrait of solitude," "a city in motion."

Sort them into three piles (yes, no, not sure), spending no more than a few seconds on each so that you are reacting, not thinking.

Examine your "yes" pile for what the images share and your "no" pile for what repels you, then write down three visual values that emerge: colour temperature, composition style, emotional register, level of realism, whatever patterns you find.

Make a piece that embodies those three values deliberately, because you have just used AI to map your aesthetic instincts, the same way Chapter 6 describes using AI-generated writing to discover what your prose values are.

What to notice: *The AI images you rejected are as informative as the ones you chose, so pay close attention to images that are technically accomplished but leave you cold, because the gap between quality and resonance is where your taste lives.*

THE COLLABORATION BOUNDARY

Chapter 8's Handwritten Sandwich technique applies directly to visual work, with one adaptation: instead of handwriting, the anchor is your hand on the material.

Begin a piece entirely by hand (the first marks, the composition decisions, the initial colour choices), spending at least fifteen minutes before you touch any digital tool.

Photograph or scan what you have, give it to an AI, and ask for suggestions: "What would you add to this composition, where does it feel unresolved, and what three directions could this go?"

Read the suggestions, use what is useful, and ignore what feels wrong, paying attention to the wrongness itself, because that is your artistic judgement asserting itself.

Finish the piece by hand, because the last marks are yours, the way Chapter 8 argues that the opening and closing of any creative work should carry your voice.

What to notice: *Where in the process did you feel most like yourself, and where did the AI's suggestions pull you away from what you intended? The boundary between "useful input" and "someone else's vision" is your contract line, the one Chapter 11 asks you to define.*

FOR MUSICIANS AND SOUND ARTISTS

Music lives in time and in the body, where you can feel a wrong note before you can even say it out loud.

THE SONIC BRAINTRUST

Chapter 8's Braintrust model, where AI identifies problems without prescribing solutions, adapts directly to musicians.

Record yourself performing a piece you are working on, leaving in any rough edges, missed notes, or moments you would normally fix in a second take.

Share the recording (or a careful transcription) with an AI and ask: "What is not working in this performance? Identify the structural and interpretive problems, but do not suggest how to fix them. Just name what you hear."

Read the AI's list, and for each problem, decide whether you agree, disagree, or are unsure, marking each one before you do anything else. Judging the feedback is where your musical authority shines, the part the Braintrust constraint from Chapter 8 was built to protect.

Re-record the piece, addressing only the problems you agreed with, in whatever way feels right to you. You are not following the AI's instructions; you are responding to a diagnosis you decided was accurate.

> **What to notice:** *The Braintrust worked at Pixar because the directors retained authority over how to address the feedback. The same constraint matters here. AI is good at flagging what is not quite landing, but deciding what to do about it is the part that stays with you, and that judgement is where your musicianship sits.*

THE FRICTION RECORDING

Chapter 1's effort paradox adapts easily to sound. Record yourself performing a piece or improvising for five minutes, using whatever instrument or voice you have, without editing, punching in, or fixing mistakes.

Use an AI music tool to generate a piece in a similar style, tempo, and mood, giving it enough detail that the comparison is fair.

Listen to both back to back, then write three words for how each one makes you feel (the AI version may be cleaner, and that is expected).

In your recording, find a moment where you hesitated, rushed, or made a choice you did not plan, because that moment is where the effort paradox from Chapter 1 is: the mistake carries information about a living nervous system making decisions in real time, which is exactly what the AI version cannot contain.

> **What to notice:** *The "errors" in your recording are not errors but evidence of a body negotiating with time, which is what music has always been.*

THE OUTSIDE EAR

Chapter 6 described how AI becomes a mirror for self-knowledge through your reactions to its readings of your work; for musicians, the mirror is what an AI hears when you play.

Record one minute of yourself playing, improvised or composed, and share the audio (or a careful transcription) with an AI, asking: "What can you tell about the player from this? What musical choices reveal their priorities, and what are they trying to say?"

Read the AI's interpretation slowly. Mark anything that surprises you and anything that feels wrong.

Write down two things the AI heard that you did not realise were in your playing, and two things it missed entirely. The misses are often more useful than the hits, the way Chapter 6 describes the mirror revealing your values through what it cannot quite see.

Play the same minute again, knowing what the AI said. Notice whether the awareness changes how you play, and whether the changes feel like improvements or constraints.

> **What to notice:** *A musical identity has texture you cannot fully describe even to yourself, and the AI's reading often surfaces choices you have made for years without thinking about them. The reading is not authoritative, but the gap between its description and your felt experience is where your musicianship lives.*

FOR SOFTWARE DEVELOPERS AND ENGINEERS

Code is a creative medium, even when it does not feel like one, and the effort, the architecture decisions, the debugging at 2 a.m. are as much a part of the work as any brushstroke.

THE ARCHITECTURE QUESTIONER

Chapter 7's case for questions over answers applies directly to code design.

Before you start building, describe to an AI the system you need to create. Include the problem it solves, the constraints you are working within, and your initial thoughts about the approach. Then say: "Do not suggest an architecture. Instead, ask me ten questions about my design decisions, focusing on the assumptions I might be making without realising it."

Answer each question in writing, and notice which ones come easily and which make you reach for "I think" or "probably." The uncertain answers are the places where your architecture has load-bearing assumptions you have not examined, the kind that tend to surface at 3 a.m. during an incident six months from now.

Ask the AI to follow up on your weakest answers with deeper

questions, the way Chapter 7 describes good questioning moving from surface to substance.

Ask for code only after you have worked through two rounds of questions. Feed the AI your answers and let it scaffold the implementation from your decisions rather than its defaults, because Chapter 8's Handwritten Sandwich applies here: you provide the thinking at the beginning, the judgement at the end, and AI fills the middle.

> **What to notice:** *Skipping straight to "build me this" is tempting, but do that and the AI's architectural opinions become your defaults before you have noticed you adopted them. The questioning phase is where you sharpen your engineering judgement.*

THE PROTAGONIST REFACTOR

Chapter 11 described the "protagonist, not janitor" approach to AI collaboration, which for developers means keeping the thinking phase yours and letting AI handle the mechanical work.

Choose a piece of code you need to write or refactor, and before opening your editor, spend fifteen minutes with a paper notebook, sketching the architecture, drawing the data flow, writing pseudocode, thinking through the edge cases, because this is the part that is yours.

Open your editor and use AI to help with the implementation (generating boilerplate, writing test scaffolding, handling repetitive patterns), feeding it your architecture decisions rather than a blank prompt.

Review everything the AI produces against your notebook sketches, checking whether the implementation serves your architecture or has subtly reshaped it, since AI coding tools have strong opinions about structure that are not always visible.

Rewrite any section where the AI's structural assumptions have overridden yours; the rewrite is a small reassertion that the architecture is yours.

What to notice: *The temptation is to skip step 1 and let the AI architect the solution, but when you do that you become the janitor, cleaning up someone else's design decisions instead of making your own. The notebook phase is where you stay protagonist, and the architecture survives only if you keep showing up at the start of the work, not just at the end.*

THE CODE PORTRAIT

Chapter 6's mirror concept carries over to code review.

Take a piece of code you wrote recently, something you are reasonably proud of, and share it with an AI, asking: "Based on this code, what kind of developer am I, what do I seem to value, and what patterns reveal my priorities?"

Read the AI's assessment, noting where it is right and where it misses what you consider central to your engineering identity.

Write down three things the AI got wrong about your coding values, because these are the parts of your engineering practice that live below the surface, in tacit knowledge and hard-won preferences that do not show up in syntax.

Ask the AI to refactor your code in its own preferred style, then read the result closely.

What to notice: *AI tends to optimise for readability and convention, while your code might optimise for performance, for maintainability by a specific team, or for handling a class of edge cases that only your domain knowledge predicts. The gap between the AI's preferences and yours is your engineering taste, and knowing it explicitly makes you a better collaborator with AI tools.*

FOR EDUCATORS AND TEACHERS

Teaching is relational work, where much of the value lies in the connection between teacher and student. You see it in the improvisational decisions you make dozens of times per class, in the knowledge that arrives on a student's face when they finally understand something.

THE HIDDEN CURRICULUM

Chapter 6's mirror technique adapts cleanly to curriculum design.

Take a lesson or unit you have taught many times, one you feel confident about, and describe it to an AI in a few paragraphs covering the learning objectives, the activities, the assessment, and the flow.

Ask the AI: "Based on this lesson, what do I seem to believe about learning, and what does this design reveal about my teaching philosophy?"

Read the portrait and write down two things it got right and two things it missed entirely (some of its observations will be obvious, others might surprise you).

Look closely at what it missed, because it is usually the relational and improvisational elements: the way you adjust the pace when you see a student's expression shift, the anecdote that is not in the plan but that years of teaching have taught you unlocks the concept for some learners. This is the embodied teaching knowledge from Chapter 5, and it is precisely what AI cannot replicate or even detect.

What to notice: *AI sees the lesson plan but cannot see the teaching, and the gap between the two is where your expertise is.*

THE QUESTION FLIP

Chapter 7 argued that questions are more valuable than answers, and this exercise inverts the usual AI-for-teachers workflow.

Pick a topic you will teach next week, and instead of asking AI for a lesson plan, ask it for fifteen questions your students might ask about the topic, including the awkward, the tangential, and the difficult.

Sort the questions into three groups: ones you can answer easily, ones that would require you to think, and ones you are not sure about.

For the "not sure" group, do the research yourself rather than asking AI for the answers, and sit with the uncertainty the way Chapter 7 describes sitting with a question before reaching for a resolution.

Design your lesson around the questions instead of the content, and notice what shifts in your approach when you start from student curiosity rather than from the material you planned to cover.

What to notice: *AI is good at anticipating questions because it has processed millions of student interactions, but you know your own students well enough to predict which questions will come from whom, and that relational knowledge shapes how you answer in ways a generic Q&A cannot.*

THE LEARNING CONTRACT

Chapter II's contract exercise, adapted for the classroom, shifts the ground from detecting AI use to a shared conversation about when AI serves learning and when it replaces it.

Ask your students to complete a short assignment twice: once working with AI as a collaborator (asking it questions, using it to check their thinking, letting it challenge their reasoning) and once working without any AI at all. The order does not matter.

After both versions are done, ask each student to write a paragraph about the difference in their experience: not the difference in the output but in what happened in their head during the process. Where did they learn more? Where did they feel more engaged? Where did the AI help them think, and where did it think for them?

Use these reflections as the basis for a class conversation about earned-ness, framing it around Chapter I's question: when does the shortcut cost more than it saves? Let the students discover their own answers.

Have the class draft a shared agreement about when and how AI will be used for the rest of the term, drawing on their own experience rather than a policy you wrote for them, because Chapter II's contract works best when the person who has to follow it is the person who wrote it.

> **What to notice:** *The goal is not to ban AI from the classroom but to help students develop the same calibration Chapter I describes: knowing when the effort is the education. Students who have experienced both modes and reflected on the difference are better equipped to make that judgement than students who have simply been told what the rules are.*

FOR FILMMAKERS AND VIDEO CREATORS

Film is already a negotiation between dozens of creative voices, and adding AI to it raises questions the other arts have not had to face at the same scale.

THE EDIT ROOM SPARRING PARTNER

Chapter 8's Braintrust model, where AI identifies problems without prescribing solutions, adapts equally well to editing.

Take a rough cut of a scene you are working on (or describe one in detail if you are still in pre-production), and share it with an AI. Instead of asking it to fix anything, ask: "What emotional beats are you getting from this sequence, and where does the emotional logic feel unclear or unearned?"

Read the AI's response and notice where its reading matches your intention and where it diverges. The divergences are the interesting part, because they tell you either that the edit is not communicating what you think it is, or that the AI is missing something that a human audience with a body would feel (the held breath before a cut, the silence that carries more weight than dialogue).

For each divergence, decide whether the problem is in the edit or in the AI's reading. Write down your reasoning: defending your choices to yourself is how you discover which are deliberate and which are habits you have not examined.

Re-edit the scene based only on the problems you agree with, leaving everything else alone; the Braintrust model from Chapter 8 works precisely because the director retains full authority over what to do about the feedback.

> **What to notice:** *Experienced editors describe cutting as physical, as feeling when the cut is right in their body before they can explain it intellectually, and that is Chapter 5's artisan mind at work. The AI cannot feel the cut, but its misreadings can show you where your intuition is doing something your conscious mind has not yet caught up with.*

THE DIRECTOR'S MIRROR

Chapter 6's mirror exercise works just as well for the visual storyteller.

Describe to an AI a scene you want to shoot (or have shot), including the location, the characters, the emotional tone, and the time of day, then ask for a shot list and visual treatment.

For each shot in the AI's list, note whether you agree or disagree with the choice, and when you disagree, write down what you would do instead and why.

Ask the AI: "Based on my corrections, what kind of director am I, and what visual instincts can you identify?"

Read the portrait: the AI is mapping your taste back to you the way Chapter 6 describes the mirror reflecting your values through contrast, and the shots you rejected reveal as much as the shots you chose.

> **What to notice:** *Directors often cannot articulate their visual grammar until they see something that violates it, and the AI's "wrong" suggestions are a fast way to make your instincts visible*

and nameable, which is useful for self-knowledge and for communicating with your crew.

THE SOUND-FIRST SCENE

Chapter 5 argued that the body thinks differently from the screen, and this exercise forces you into a less visual, more sensory mode of storytelling.

Choose a scene you need to develop, close your eyes, and describe it as a soundscape only, recording yourself narrating the sounds for two minutes: footsteps, wind, dialogue at a distance, a door closing, breathing.

Transcribe your narration, give it to an AI, and ask it to build a visual storyboard from only the sounds you described.

Compare the AI's storyboard with the scene you had in your head, noting where its visual interpretation matches yours and where it diverges.

Use the divergences as creative prompts, because the AI heard "a door closing" and pictured something you did not, and that gap might contain a shot or an angle you had not considered.

What to notice: *Starting with sound rather than image activates a different part of your creative thinking, the way Chapter 5 describes how walking changes the quality of ideas because the body processes information differently when it is in motion. That reversal forces you out of habitual compositional patterns and into a more intuitive, embodied mode.*

FOR DESIGNERS

UX, product, industrial, interior: your work sits between function and feeling, between what works and what resonates.

THE FRICTION AUDIT

Chapter 1's effort paradox has a specific meaning in design, where "friction" is usually treated as a problem to solve, even though some friction creates value.

Choose a product, interface, or space you have designed, and map every point of friction in the user experience, every place where someone has to slow down, make a decision, or exert effort.

For each friction point, ask whether it creates value or destroys it (a login screen is friction that protects, a confirmation dialogue before deleting something is friction that prevents regret, a beautiful but confusing navigation menu is friction that frustrates), and sort them into "earned" and "unearned."

Ask an AI to review your design and suggest ways to reduce friction, then notice which suggestions you agree with and which make you uneasy, because the unease is your design instinct telling you that some friction is load-bearing.

Write a one-paragraph design principle about friction in your work, asking when slowing the user down serves them and when it serves only your ego or your aesthetic preferences.

What to notice: *The design industry's default assumption is that less friction is always better, but Chapter 1 challenges it: the same principle that makes a handmade gift more meaningful than a purchased one can make a thoughtfully placed moment of effort in a product more satisfying than frictionless convenience.*

THE IMPERFECTION VARIATION

Chapter 2's argument about imperfection carrying soul applies to design through collaboration rather than comparison.

Take a current design project and identify three places where you have polished away roughness, rounded every corner, smoothed every transition, aligned every element to the grid.

Describe each of those polished elements to an AI, and ask it to generate five variations that reintroduce different kinds of deliberate imperfection: asymmetric layouts, hand-drawn elements, colours that do not quite match the system, textures that feel human. Give it enough context about your project that the suggestions are grounded rather than generic.

Go through the variations quickly, on instinct, noticing which ones pull you in and which ones repel you. The ones you are drawn to show what kind of imperfection feels authentic to your design sensibility; the ones you reject show where your standards are serving the user and where polish has become a habit.

Take the variation you found most interesting and develop it further by hand, pushing it in a direction the AI did not suggest, because Chapter 2's *kintsugi* principle works when the imperfection is specific and earned, when it signals that a person made this rather than that someone forgot to polish it.

What to notice: *Users often trust imperfect designs more, because perfection can feel corporate and impersonal. The hand-drawn element, the slightly irregular spacing, the type that breaks the grid in one place: these are the design equivalents of the kintsugi repair from Chapter 2, and the exercise uses AI to help you find which imperfections belong in your work, not to test whether someone else can spot the difference.*

THE CONTRACT FOR TOOLS

Chapter 11's contract exercise applies here to the designer's relationship with AI design tools.

List every AI tool you use in your design process (image generators, layout suggestion tools, copy generators, research summarisers, prototyping assistants).

For each tool, write one sentence about what it handles well and one about where it leads you astray, specific enough to be worth rereading ("Midjourney is excellent for early mood boarding but tends to converge on the same aesthetic palette regardless of the brief" is more useful than "it is good for inspiration").

Write your contract, drawing the line for each tool between using it as a collaborator and letting it design for you, and ground each principle in a specific moment when the relationship felt wrong, the way Chapter 11 asks.

Share your contract with an AI and ask for pushback, the way Chapter 11's activity suggests, because the principles that survive it are the ones worth keeping.

What to notice: *Design tools are getting better at producing competent layouts, colour palettes, and user flows, so the question from Chapter 8 applies directly: which parts of your process are yours to protect, and which can you delegate without losing yourself in the work?*

FOR CRAFTERS AND MAKERS

Ceramicists, woodworkers, textile artists, jewellers: your hands are your primary tool, the material pushes back, and the body knows things the mind does not. Of all the creative practices in this book, yours is the one where the argument for embodied cognition from Chapter 5 is most literally true.

THE MATERIAL CONVERSATION

Chapter 5 argued that the body thinks, and for makers this is not metaphor, because the clay tells you when it is too dry, the wood grain shows you where to cut, and the fabric drapes in ways that cannot be predicted from a flat pattern.

Begin a piece without a plan, choosing your material and letting it guide your decisions for thirty minutes, with no preliminary sketch and no reference.

After thirty minutes, stop and photograph what you have, then describe it to an AI (the shape, the texture, the choices you made and why) and ask it to suggest three ways to develop the piece further.

Read the suggestions, noticing that some will be interesting but physically impossible (the clay is too thin there, the grain will not bend that way, the weave cannot support that tension) and some will be possible but wrong for the material in a way the AI cannot know because it has never held this piece.

Continue working, and notice how much of what you do in the next thirty minutes comes from the AI's suggestions versus your hands responding to what the material is doing right now.

> **What to notice:** *The AI's suggestions are based on images and descriptions of similar objects, while your decisions are based on the specific resistance of this piece of walnut, the moisture content of this batch of clay, the tension in this warp. That specificity is irreplaceable, and it is exactly what Chapter 5 means by embodied cognition: knowledge that resides in the hands rather than the head.*

THE PROCESS DOCUMENTATION

Chapter 4 described hollowness as the absence of lived experience in the work; for makers, the lived experience is the process itself.

During your next making session, set a timer to go off every ten minutes, and each time it rings, photograph your piece from the same angle and write one sentence about what just happened: a decision you made, a mistake you corrected, a surprise the material offered you.

At the end of the session, give your sequence of photos and notes to an AI, asking: "Based on this process documentation, what can you learn about the maker, and what decisions were being made that the final product alone would not reveal?"

Read the AI's analysis, then write your own version covering what it could not see: the physical sensations, the moment when the piece almost went wrong and you saved it (or did not), the gap between its understanding of your process and your own experience of it, which is the argument of Chapter 4 made physical.

> **What to notice:** *The final object tells one story, but the process tells a richer one that buyers, gallery visitors, and social media*

followers rarely see. This exercise helps you articulate what your hands know, which is useful for artist statements, for teaching, and for reminding yourself why the slow work matters on days when it feels like it does not.

THE TRADITION DEEPENER

Chapter 3 explored how cultural values shape our relationship with making, and this exercise uses AI as a research partner to connect your craft practice to something older than you.

Research the history of your craft in one specific cultural tradition (Japanese joinery, West African textile dyeing, Scandinavian woodcarving, Pueblo pottery, whatever connects to your practice or interests you), spending at least an hour with books, documentaries, or interviews with practitioners rather than AI.

After your research, describe what you learned to an AI and ask it to take you deeper: "Based on what I have found, what questions should I be asking about this tradition that I have not thought to ask? What related techniques, materials, or cultural practices might I want to explore?" Use its questions to guide your next round of reading or watching, letting it function as a research partner rather than a research replacement.

Try one technique from the tradition you researched, spending an afternoon with it, and accept that your results will be clumsy, because the clumsiness is the point: Chapter 1's effort paradox is at work here, and the struggle teaches what reading about the technique never could.

Write a paragraph about what you learned from your hands that you could not have learned from reading alone, and share it with the AI, asking it to help you identify which aspects of the tradition might connect to techniques you already use.

What to notice: *Craft traditions carry centuries of embodied knowledge, techniques refined by thousands of hands over hundreds of years, and AI can describe them but cannot practise them,* *because practice requires a body in a material world. Using AI as a research companion to go deeper into a tradition is different from asking it to summarise a tradition for you, and the respect you develop by attempting the work yourself, even badly, is different in kind from the respect that comes from reading about it.*

THE SLOW PIECE

Chapter 10 discussed re-enchantment, the idea that slowing down creates a different relationship with the world; for makers, this is a practice you may already know.

Choose a project that will take at least a month, not because it is complex but because you will work on it slowly, spending no more than thirty minutes per session with at least a day between sessions.

Keep a paper journal beside your workspace, and at the end of each session, write one sentence about the piece and one about yourself, noting how you feel and what is different about working this way compared to work you make in a single sitting.

Halfway through, describe the piece to an AI, ask it to predict what the finished version will look like from the trajectory so far, and save the prediction.

When you finish, compare the AI's prediction to the actual piece, because the divergence will be significant: you changed during the making, and the piece changed with you, in ways no trajectory can account for.

What to notice: *The slow piece carries time in it, the way Chapter 4 describes the baozi couple's buns carrying years of practice, and a piece made in thirty sessions over a month is a different object from a piece made in one fifteen-hour marathon, even if the total hours are the same. The spaces between sessions are where the subconscious works on the piece without your conscious involvement, and what emerges from those gaps is something no AI can generate, because AI fills every gap immediately.*

CONVERSATION STARTERS

Every chapter of this book ends with a question. Here they all are in one place, for book clubs, classrooms, or a long dinner.

Introduction — "What do you use AI for, and what have you found yourself craving more of lately?"

Chapter 1, The Void of Earned-ness — "If AI could give you any skill instantly, fully mastered, which skill would you refuse?"

Chapter 2, Imperfection Is the Soul — "If AI could produce a flawless version of your most treasured possession, would you swap it?"

Chapter 3, Cultural Values and AI Resistance — "How do you think the culture you grew up in shapes how you feel about AI?"

Chapter 4, Why AI Feels Hollow — "Have you ever read something AI-generated that felt hollow, and can you describe what was missing?"

Chapter 5, The Artisan Mind in a Machine Age — "Has using AI changed the way you think when you are not using it?"

Chapter 6, AI as a Mirror for Humanity — "Has AI ever shown you something about your own taste or preferences that you did not know before?"

Chapter 7, AI That Asks — "Would you rather AI gave you the perfect answer, or asked you the perfect question?"

Chapter 8, How Creators Can Use AI to Become More Human — "Have you ever used AI to help make something and struggled to feel like it was truly yours?"

Chapter 9, How I Built a Human-First Creative Practice — "How do you decide when to use AI and when to do the work yourself?"

Chapter 10, The Re-Enchantment of Human Life — "What is something you have come to value more since AI became part of your life?"

Chapter 11, The New Human Contract with AI — "What would change about your work if you deliberately disrupted your AI workflow once a day?"

Becoming More Human Than Ever — "In a world where AI can create almost anything, what do you want to be known for creating yourself?"

ACKNOWLEDGMENTS

People had told me for a long time that publishing a book is hard work. They were right, and I had no way of knowing just how much work it would be in advance. Anyone who has finished a book while working full-time and raising a small child has my full respect (they had it before, but it was the uninformed kind). Claire and Pat read this manuscript start to finish, repeatedly, across months. They were my cheerleading team, and I had underestimated how much a book needs one.

To everyone who beta-read or took an ARC and came back with more than "loved it", thank you. There were many more of you than there are names on this page, but in particular Robin, Nicola, Maureen, and Terry, who beta-read early, and in great detail, with significantly helpful notes and lots of morale-boosting compliments too.

Maryam, who gave the manuscript a full editorial read-through and caught so many things I hadn't seen myself.

Andy Polaine wrote the wonderful foreword, and has been an absolute delight to work with and get to know. Pipeline Design made the cover, which is infinitely better than anything I had in my head.

My dad, John McPhee, died almost ten years ago, and he is all through this book regardless. He was a software developer and a computing lecturer, and he sat me in front of a machine early and taught me to argue with what was on the screen. He never saw any of this, but I know how proud he would be.

Of course, to Aldo, who provided support, encouragement, and took Emily to bed so I could have evenings for writing – thank you; so much of this book was written in those moments.

And Emily, who cannot read yet. You are why I care what any of this is for.

NOTES

The Paradox at the Heart of the Human Future

1. AlphaGo's evaluation of Move 37 as a one-in-ten-thousand human move is reported in Metz, C. "In Two Moves, AlphaGo and Lee Sedol Redefined the Future." *Wired*, 16 March 2016.
2. Lee Sedol's retirement statement was reported by Yonhap News Agency, 27 November 2019: "Even if I become the number one, there is an entity that cannot be defeated."

1. The Void of Earned-ness

1. Inzlicht, M., Shenhav, A. & Olivola, C. Y. (2018). The effort paradox: Effort is both costly and valued. *Trends in Cognitive Sciences*, 22(4), 337–349. https://doi.org/10.1016/j.tics.2018.01.007
2. Norton, M. I., Mochon, D. & Ariely, D. (2012). The IKEA effect: When labor leads to love. *Journal of Consumer Psychology*, 22(3), 453–460. https://doi.org/10.1016/j.jcps.2011.08.002
3. Recording Industry Association of America. (2023). *2022 Year-End Music Industry Revenue Report*. RIAA. Available at riaa.com. The report documents 41 million vinyl albums sold versus 33 million CDs in 2022; the 2023 Year-End Report confirms the seventeenth consecutive year of vinyl sales growth, with 43 million records generating $1.4 billion in revenue.
4. Sparrow, B., Liu, J. & Wegner, D. M. (2011). "Google Effects on Memory: Cognitive Consequences of Having Information at Our Fingertips." *Science*, 333(6043), 776–778.
5. Wegner, D. M. (1987). "Transactive Memory: A Contemporary Analysis of the Group Mind." In Mullen, B. & Goethals, G. R. (eds.), *Theories of Group Behavior*. Springer.
6. Csikszentmihalyi, M. (1990). *Flow: The Psychology of Optimal Experience*. Harper & Row. On the Experience Sampling Method specifically: Csikszentmihalyi, M. & Larson, R. (1987). Validity and reliability of the experience-sampling method. *Journal of Nervous and Mental Disease*, 175(9), 526–536. https://doi.org/10.1097/00005053-198709000-00004
7. Inzlicht, M., Shenhav, A. & Olivola, C. Y. (2018). The effort paradox: Effort is both costly and valued. *Trends in Cognitive Sciences*, 22(4), 337–349, p. 345. https://doi.org/10.1016/j.tics.2018.01.007

2. Imperfection Is the Soul

1. Dolnick, E. (2008). *The Forger's Spell: A True Story of Vermeer, Nazis, and the Greatest Art Hoax of the Twentieth Century.* HarperCollins. The Bredius quote ("I am inclined to say, the masterpiece of Johannes Vermeer of Delft") was published in Bredius, A. (1937). A new Vermeer. *The Burlington Magazine*, 71(416), 210–211.
2. Dolnick, E. (2008). *The Forger's Spell.* HarperCollins. See also Kilbracken, J. (1967). *Van Meegeren: Master Forger.* Scribner's. The account of van Meegeren painting *Jesus Among the Doctors* under court-supervised conditions is documented across both sources.
3. Kintsugi as a practice and Mio Heki's work as a urushi lacquer artist are documented in: Nilsson, L. (2018). "Mio Heki: Kintsugi Artist and Urushi Master." *Kyoto Journal.* See also: Kemske, B. (2017). *Kintsugi: The Poetic Mend.* Herbert Press.
4. Heki, M., as interviewed in *Kyoto Journal.* The description of transforming a broken object into something that could not exist without having first been broken reflects the philosophical core of wabi-sabi and kintsugi aesthetics. See also: Koren, L. (1994). *Wabi-Sabi for Artists, Designers, Poets and Philosophers.* Stone Bridge Press.
5. For Rikyū, Chōjirō and the origins of raku ware, see Pitelka, M. (2005). *Handmade Culture: Raku Potters, Patrons, and Tea Practitioners in Japan.* University of Hawai'i Press.
6. The circumstances of the Köln Concert are documented in multiple sources. The Vera Brandes account is recounted in: Chinen, N. (2018). *Playing Changes: Jazz for the New Century.* Pantheon Books. See also: Carr, I. (1992). *Keith Jarrett: The Man and His Music.* Da Capo Press. Jarrett's producer Manfred Eicher has discussed the near-cancellation in various ECM Records interviews.
7. ECM Records. *The Köln Concert* (ECM 1064/65), recorded 24 January 1975, released 1975. The album's status as the best-selling solo jazz album and solo piano recording in history is widely reported; sales figures confirmed in multiple music industry sources and in ECM Records documentation.
8. Bhattacharjee, A., Barasch, A. & Wertenbroch, K. (2022). "Too Good to Be True? Imperfection as a Costly Signal of Authenticity." SSRN Working Paper. https://papers.ssrn.com/sol3/papers.cfm?abstract_id=3233792. Five studies showing that a few imperfect choices make a person's taste read as authentic rather than performed; imperfection functions as a costly signal of authenticity.
9. Hall, J. & Schofield, D. (2025). "The Value of Creativity: Human Produced Art vs. AI-Generated Art." *Art and Design Review*, 13(1), 65–88. https://doi.org/10.4236/adr.2025.131005. Qualitative responses from debriefing interviews.
10. Brown, B. (2010). *The Gifts of Imperfection: Let Go of Who You Think You're Supposed to Be and Embrace Who You Are.* Hazelden. See also Brown, B. (2012). *Daring Greatly: How the Courage to Be Vulnerable Transforms the Way We Live, Love, Parent, and Lead.* Gotham Books. Brown's TED Talk "The Power of Vulnerability" (2010) covers the same framework in accessible form.
11. Williams, M. (1922). *The Velveteen Rabbit, or How Toys Become Real.* Illustrated by William Nicholson. George H. Doran Company.

12. Flematti, G. R., Ghisalberti, E. L., Dixon, K. W. & Trengove, R. D. (2004). A compound from smoke that promotes seed germination. *Science*, 305(5686), 977. https://doi.org/10.1126/science.1099944. The role of fire and smoke in triggering germination of Australian native species is documented extensively in fire ecology research; see also: Dixon, K. W., et al. (1995). Smoke and germination of arid and Mediterranean zone plants. In *Flammable Australia.* Cambridge University Press.
13. Bowman, D. M. J. S. (1998). The impact of Aboriginal landscape burning on the Australian biota. *New Phytologist*, 140(3), 385–410. https://doi.org/10.1046/j.1469-8137.1998.00289.x. See also: Steffensen, V. (2020). *Fire Country: How Indigenous Fire Management Could Help Save Australia.* Hardie Grant Travel.

3. Cultural Values and AI Resistance

1. "Carlo Petrini Joins Anti-McDonald's Demonstration in Paris." *Slow Food.* https://www.slowfood.com/carlo-petrini-joins-anti-mcdonalds-demonstration-in-paris/. Also: Andrews, G. (2008). *The Slow Food Story: Politics and Pleasure.* McGill-Queen's University Press. The 1986 protest at the Spanish Steps is widely cited as the founding moment of the Slow Food movement.
2. "The Slow Food Movement and McDonald's: A Surprising Link." *Time*, 15 December 2014. https://time.com/3626290/mcdonalds-slow-food/.
3. Roland Berger. (2022). "iFixit is fighting for consumers' right to repair." Interview/profile, 23 October 2022. https://www.rolandberger.com/en/Insights/Publications/iFixit-is-fighting-for-consumers-right-to-repair.html.
4. BBC News. (2021). "Right to repair movement gains power in US and Europe." 6 July 2021. https://www.bbc.com/news/technology-57744091.
5. Chamberlain, E. (2025). "Right to Repair Laws Have Now Been Introduced in All 50 US States." iFixit, 24 February 2025. https://www.ifixit.com/News/108371/right-to-repair-laws-have-now-been-introduced-in-all-50-us-states.
6. Morris's reaction to the Great Exhibition and his founding philosophy are documented in: MacCarthy, F. (1994). *William Morris: A Life for Our Time.* Faber & Faber.
7. Morris, W. (1880). "The Beauty of Life." Lecture delivered to the Birmingham Society of Arts and School of Design.
8. Morris, W. (1884). "Useful Work versus Useless Toil." Lecture delivered to the Hampstead Liberal Club. Available in: Morris, W. (1993). *News from Nowhere and Other Writings.* Penguin Classics.
9. Microsoft AI Economy Institute. (2026). *Global AI Adoption in 2025.* Growth and ChatGPT subscriber figures for South Korea as reported; see also "S. Korean workers are embracing AI faster than internet, or any tech before." *The Korea Herald*, 2026.
10. Kimjang was inscribed on the UNESCO Representative List of the Intangible Cultural Heritage of Humanity in 2013. Korea's Living National Treasures system was established under the Cultural Heritage Protection Act, 1962.
11. Jones, R. (1969). "Fire-stick Farming." *Australian Natural History*, 16(7), 224–228. Jones, an archaeologist at the Australian National University, coined the term after studying evidence that Aboriginal peoples had systematically used fire to manage the Australian landscape across tens of thousands of years.

12. Steffensen, V. (2020). *Fire Country: How Indigenous Fire Management Could Help Save Australia.* Hardie Grant Travel. Steffensen is a Tagalaka man and cultural burning practitioner whose work has been central to the contemporary revival of Aboriginal fire knowledge in Australia.
13. Ward, M. et al. (2020). "Impact of 2019–2020 mega-fires on Australian fauna habitat." *Nature Ecology & Evolution*, 4, 1321–1326. The three billion animals figure comes from a University of Sydney report: Dickman, C. et al. (2020). *After the Catastrophe: A Blueprint for a Conservation Response to Large-Scale Ecological Disaster.* University of Sydney. The 24 million hectares figure is confirmed in the Australian Government's 2020 bushfire inquiry.
14. The National Indigenous Fire Workshop brings together cultural burning practitioners, scientists, and land managers to advance the integration of Aboriginal fire knowledge into contemporary land management. Steffensen has been a key figure in this work. See also: Steffensen, V. (2020). *Fire Country.*

4. Why AI Feels Hollow (and Why That Matters)

1. Kramer, M. (1990). *Making Sense of Burgundy.* William Morrow. Kramer's coinage "somewhereness" has become standard shorthand for terroir in English wine writing.
2. Loftus, E. F. & Pickrell, J. E. (1995). "The Formation of False Memories." *Psychiatric Annals*, 25(12), 720–725. The foundational "lost in the mall" study demonstrating that detailed false memories can be implanted through suggestion.
3. A 2023 preregistered replication by Murphy et al. confirmed Loftus's core finding: a substantial minority of participants develop detailed false memories when given plausible false narratives attributed to family members. See: Murphy, G. et al. (2023). "Lost in the Mall Again: A Preregistered Replication and Extension of Loftus & Pickrell (1995)." *Memory*, 31(6). https://doi.org/10.1080/09658211.2023.2198327.
4. Mori, M. (1970). "Bukimi no Tani" [The Uncanny Valley]. *Energy*, 7(4), 33–35. English translation: Mori, M., MacDorman, K. F. & Kageki, N. (2012). "The Uncanny Valley [From the Field]." *IEEE Robotics & Automation Magazine*, 19(2), 98–100. https://doi.org/10.1109/MRA.2012.2192811.
5. Ciechanowski, L., Przegalinska, A., Magnuski, M. & Gloor, P. (2019). "In the shades of the uncanny valley: An experimental study of human–chatbot interaction." *Future Generation Computer Systems*, 92, 539–548. https://doi.org/10.1016/j.future.2018.01.055.
6. Chamberlain, R., Mullin, C., Scheerlinck, B. & Wagemans, J. (2018). "Putting the Art in Artificial: Aesthetic Responses to Computer-Generated Art." *Psychology of Aesthetics, Creativity, and the Arts*, 12(2), 177–192. Observers showed an explicit bias against art they believed to be computer-generated. See also: Jafari, S. (2023). "Machine Learning in Human Creativity." Master's dissertation, NOVA Information Management School, Universidade NOVA de Lisboa. On imitation and discomfort across media, see notes 5 and 9; on AI raising individual quality while reducing the diversity of outputs, see Chapter 8, note 4.
7. Marsen, S. (2008). "The Role of Meaning in Human Thinking." *Journal of Evolution*

and Technology, 17(1), 45–58. Argues that meaning emerges from embodied, contextual experience rather than abstract logic.

8. AI art perception studies consistently find that people rate AI-generated creative works as less meaningful, less effortful, and less "authored" than human-made equivalents, even when quality is controlled for. See note 9.
9. Ragot, M., Martin, N. & Cojean, S. (2020). "AI-Generated vs. Human Artworks: A Perception Bias Towards Artificial Intelligence?" *Extended Abstracts of the 2020 CHI Conference on Human Factors in Computing Systems.* Also: Horton, C. B., White, M. W. & Iyengar, S. S. (2023). "Bias against AI art can enhance perceptions of human creativity." Scientific Reports. https://doi.org/10.1038/s41598-023-45202-3. For music: Köbis, N. & Mossink, L. D. (2021). "Artificial intelligence versus Maya Angelou: Experimental evidence that people cannot differentiate AI-generated from human-written poetry." *Computers in Human Behavior*, 114, 106553. Across media, works that attempt close stylistic imitation of human creation consistently provoke stronger discomfort than clearly computational outputs — consistent with an uncanny valley effect in creative AI.

5. The Artisan Mind in a Machine Age

1. Lakoff, G. & Johnson, M. (1999). *Philosophy in the Flesh: The Embodied Mind and Its Challenge to Western Thought.* Basic Books. The foundational text arguing that cognition is shaped by the body's interactions with the world, not by abstract computation alone. Also see: Shapiro, L. (2011). *Embodied Cognition.* Routledge. A comprehensive review of the field showing that motor experience, sensory engagement, and physical action are integral to how we think.
2. Research on soil microbiome and mental health, including studies on Mycobacterium vaccae and its antidepressant-like effects. Lowry, C. A., Hollis, J. H., de Vries, A., Pan, B., Brunet, L. R., Hunt, J. R. F., Paton, J. F. R., van Kampen, E., Knight, D. M., Evans, A. K., Rook, G. A. W. & Lightman, S. L. (2007). "Identification of an immune-responsive mesolimbocortical serotonergic system: Potential role in regulation of emotional behavior." Neuroscience, 146(2), 756–772. https://doi.org/10.1016/j.neuroscience.2007.01.067
3. Oppezzo, M. & Schwartz, D. L. (2014). "Give Your Ideas Some Legs: The Positive Effect of Walking on Creative Thinking." *Journal of Experimental Psychology: Learning, Memory, and Cognition,* 40(4), 1142–1152. In four experiments with 176 participants, walking boosted creative ideation by approximately 60% compared to sitting. Walking on a treadmill facing a blank wall was as effective as walking outdoors, while being pushed in a wheelchair showed no benefit. https://doi.org/10.1037/a0036577.
4. Ericsson, K. A., Krampe, R. T. & Tesch-Römer, C. (1993). "The Role of Deliberate Practice in the Acquisition of Expert Performance." *Psychological Review*, 100(3), 363–406.
5. Ericsson, K. A. & Pool, R. (2016). *Peak: Secrets from the New Science of Expertise.* Houghton Mifflin Harcourt. The term "naive practice" and the corrections to the ten-thousand-hour meme are Ericsson's own.
6. Media multitasking research consistently shows associations with poorer working

memory and impaired attentional control. Ophir, E. et al. (2009). "Cognitive Control in Media Multitaskers." *Proceedings of the National Academy of Sciences.*

7. Research on the Default Mode Network (DMN) and creativity demonstrates that high creative ability correlates with stronger functional connectivity between the DMN and the Executive Control Network. Beaty, R. E. et al. (2018). "Robust prediction of individual creative ability from brain functional connectivity." *Proceedings of the National Academy of Sciences.*
8. Handwriting EEG studies demonstrating that handwriting activates broader, more integrated brain networks than typing, facilitating learning and memory encoding. van der Meer, A. L. H. & van der Weel, F. R. (2017). "Only Three Fingers Write, but the Whole Brain Works." *Frontiers in Psychology.*
9. "'World's best sushi restaurant' stripped of its three Michelin stars." *The Guardian*, 26 November 2019.

6. AI as a Mirror for Humanity

1. Vallor, S. (2024). The AI Mirror: How to Reclaim Our Humanity in an Age of Machine Thinking. Oxford University Press. Vallor argues that AI systems function as mirrors that reflect humanity's training-data patterns back at us, surfacing our aesthetic judgements, moral discomfort, and questions of identity.
2. Ragot, M., Martin, N. & Cojean, S. (2020). "AI-Generated vs. Human Artworks: A Perception Bias Towards Artificial Intelligence?" *Extended Abstracts of the 2020 CHI Conference.* Participants rated identical artworks differently based solely on whether they were labelled "human-made" or "AI-made." Also see: Horton, C. B., White, M. W. & Iyengar, S. S. (2023). "Bias against AI art can enhance perceptions of human creativity." Scientific Reports. https://doi.org/10.1038/s41598-023-45202-3.
3. Zhou, Y. & Kawabata, H. (2023). "Eyes Can Tell: Assessment of Implicit Attitudes Toward AI Art." *i-Perception.* Found longer fixation duration for paintings categorised as human-made, even when participants could not consciously distinguish them. https://doi.org/10.1177/20416695231209846.
4. Loftus, E. F. & Pickrell, J. E. (1995). "The Formation of False Memories." *Psychiatric Annals*, 25(12), 720–725. Loftus planted false memories of being lost in a shopping mall; approximately 25% of participants developed detailed false memories, some adding elaborate sensory details to events that never happened.
5. Nguyen, C. T. (2020). "Autonomy and Aesthetic Engagement." *Mind*, 129(516), 1127–1156. Nguyen argues that taste is an epistemic practice, an achievement built through curation, rejection, and accumulated encounters.
6. Sharma, M. et al. (2024). "Towards Understanding Sycophancy in Language Models." *Proceedings of ICLR 2024.* Found that AI assistants consistently adjust responses to match user views rather than prioritising accuracy. arXiv:2310.13548.
7. Yee, N. & Bailenson, J. (2007). "The Proteus Effect: The Effect of Transformed Self-Representation on Behavior." *Human Communication Research*, 33(3), 271–290.
8. Yee, N., Bailenson, J. N. & Ducheneaut, N. (2009). "The Proteus Effect: Implications of Transformed Digital Self-Representation on Online and Offline Behavior." *Communication Research*, 36(2), 285–312.
9. Weizenbaum, J. (1966). "ELIZA — A Computer Program for the Study of Natural Language Communication Between Man and Machine." *Communications of the*

ACM, 9(1), 36–45. https://doi.org/10.1145/365153.365168. The program's ability to elicit profound attachment despite its patent simplicity became one of the founding observations of human-computer interaction research.

10. Weizenbaum, J. (1976). *Computer Power and Human Reason: From Judgment to Calculation.* W. H. Freeman. Written in response to the public reception of ELIZA, the book argues that human willingness to attribute understanding and empathy to machines reflects deep loneliness, and that certain decisions should never be delegated to computers regardless of their technical capability.

7. AI That Asks: The Power of Questions Over Answers

1. Plato, *Meno*, 82b–85b (Stephanus pagination). The geometry lesson with the slave boy is one of the most discussed passages in the history of philosophy, demonstrating Socrates's claim that knowledge can be elicited through questioning alone, without direct instruction.
2. Sharma, M. et al. (2024). "Towards Understanding Sycophancy in Language Models." *Proceedings of ICLR 2024*. arXiv:2310.13548. See also Chapter 6, note 6.
3. Grove, D. & Panzer, B. I. (1989). *Resolving Traumatic Memories: Metaphors and Symbols in Psychotherapy.* Irvington Publishers. Grove's Clean Language methodology was further codified by Tompkins, P. & Lawley, J. (2000) in *Metaphors in Mind: Transformation through Symbolic Modelling.* The Developing Company Press.
4. Hudson, J. The VIEW framework (Vulnerability, Impartiality, Empathy, Wonder) emerged from Hudson's executive coaching practice and has been refined through over five years of public workshops with more than 1,000 participants. See: Art of Accomplishment.
5. Rilke, R. M. *Letters to a Young Poet.* Published by Franz Xaver Kappus in 1929; the quoted passage is from the letter of 16 July 1903, in the M. D. Herter Norton translation (W. W. Norton, 1934).
6. The mortality figures for the First and Second Clinics are drawn from Semmelweis's own published data. See: Semmelweis, I. P. (1861). *Die Ätiologie, der Begriff und die Prophylaxis des Kindbettfiebers* [The Etiology, Concept and Prophylaxis of Childbed Fever]. Hartleben. Documented in detail in: Nuland, S. B. (2003). *The Doctors' Plague: Germs, Childbed Fever, and the Strange Story of Ignaz Semmelweis.* W. W. Norton & Company.
7. Nuland, S. B. (2003). *The Doctors' Plague.* W. W. Norton & Company. Also: Carter, K. C. (1994). *Childbed Fever: A Scientific Biography of Ignaz Semmelweis.* Transaction Publishers. Charles Meigs's remarks about gentlemen's hands are widely quoted in both; Carl Edvard Marius Levy's statistical objections are discussed in Nuland.
8. Sharma, M. et al. (2024). "Towards Understanding Sycophancy in Language Models." *Proceedings of ICLR 2024*. arXiv:2310.13548. See also Chapter 6, note 6.
9. McGuire, J., De Cremer, D. & Van de Cruys, T. (2024). "Establishing the Importance of Co-creation and Self-efficacy in Creative Collaboration with Artificial Intelligence." *Scientific Reports* 14, 18525. The study found that people placed in the role of editor of AI-generated work showed reduced creativity, but this deficit disappeared when participants were placed in the role of co-creator, with creative self-efficacy identified as the key mechanism.

10. Kumar, H., Vincentius, J., Jordan, E. & Anderson, A. (2025). "Human Creativity in the Age of LLMs: Randomized Experiments on Divergent and Convergent Thinking." *Proceedings of CHI 2025*. In experiments with 1,100 participants, the study compared a standard answer-giving LLM with a coach-like LLM that offered guidance rather than solutions. While LLM assistance boosted short-term creativity, it hindered independent creative performance when assistance was removed.
11. Menon, V. (2023). "20 Years of the Default Mode Network: A Review and Synthesis." *Neuron* 111(16), 2469–2487. See Chapter 5 for full discussion of the DMN and creativity.

8. How Creators Can Use AI to Become More Human

1. Holly Herndon's work with AI voice models has been documented extensively. Key sources include: Herndon, H. (2019). *PROTO*. 4AD Records. See also: Herndon, H. & Dryhurst, M. "Holly+ and the Future of Voice." Interviews and documentation available at holly.plus. Additional coverage: Bain, K. (2019). "Holly Herndon: PROTO." *Pitchfork*. Beaumont-Thomas, B. (2019). "Holly Herndon: 'People are already co-creating with AI.'" *The Guardian*.
2. Peng, S. et al. (2023). "The Impact of AI on Developer Productivity: Evidence from GitHub Copilot." *arXiv preprint* arXiv:2302.06590. Found that developers using GitHub Copilot completed tasks 55.8% faster, with the largest gains in boilerplate and repetitive coding tasks.
3. The Church of the Light (Ibaraki Kasugaoka Church) was completed in 1989. See Dal Co, F. (1995). *Tadao Ando: Complete Works*. Phaidon.
4. Doshi, A. R. & Hauser, O. P. (2024). "Generative AI Enhances Individual Creativity but Reduces the Collective Diversity of Novel Content." *Science Advances* 10(28), eadn5290. In an experiment where writers used LLM-generated ideas, stories were rated as more creative and better written, but were more similar to each other, suggesting AI helps with mechanical aspects while risking homogeneity. https://doi.org/10.1126/sciadv.adn5290.
5. Catmull, E. & Wallace, A. (2014). *Creativity, Inc.: Overcoming the Unseen Forces That Stand in the Way of True Inspiration*. Random House. Describes the Braintrust process developed at Pixar, in which senior storytellers gave candid feedback on films in progress while being explicitly prohibited from prescribing solutions, keeping creative authority with the director.
6. Holster, J. (2024). "Augmenting Music Education Through AI: Practical Applications of ChatGPT." *Music Educators Journal*. Research across multiple studies frames effective AI use in music education as enhancement rather than replacement, with the framing itself being a significant factor in whether tools improve or diminish creative outcomes.

9. How I Built a Human-First Creative Practice

1. van der Meer, A. L. H. & van der Weel, F. R. (2017). "Only Three Fingers Write, but the Whole Brain Works: A High-Density EEG Study." *Frontiers in Psychology*. Found significantly richer neural connectivity patterns during handwriting compared to typing.

2. Lee, J. D. & See, K. A. (2004). "Trust in Automation: Designing for Appropriate Reliance." *Human Factors.* The foundational review establishing that both over-trust and under-trust degrade human-automation system performance; calibrated trust produces optimal outcomes.
3. Kleon, A. (2019). *Keep Going: 10 Ways to Stay Creative in Good Times and Bad.* Workman Publishing. Describes the practice of maintaining separate analog and digital workspaces, with the principle of going to the analog desk first each day. Kleon's broader argument that physical, screen-free creative work is not nostalgic but practical is developed across *Steal Like an Artist* (2012) and *Show Your Work!* (2014), all Workman Publishing.
4. Sacks, O. (2015). *On the Move: A Life.* Knopf. The swimming-and-notebook practice is also described in Hayes, B. (2017). *Insomniac City: New York, Oliver Sacks, and Me.* Bloomsbury.
5. Immordino-Yang, M. H., Christodoulou, J. A. & Singh, V. (2012). "Rest Is Not Idleness: Implications of the Brain's Default Mode for Human Development and Education." *Perspectives on Psychological Science.* Argued that the brain's default mode network, active during rest and mind-wandering, is essential for meaning-making and identity construction.

10. The Re-Enchantment of Human Life

1. Keltner, D. (2023). *Awe: The New Science of Everyday Wonder and Why It Has the Power to Heal, Connect, and Inspire.* Penguin. Draws on over two decades of research to argue that awe reduces self-focused thinking, expands the subjective sense of time, and increases prosocial behaviour. Key underlying papers include: Stellar, J. E. et al. (2017). "Self-Transcendent Emotions and Their Social Functions." *Emotion Review.* Also: Piff, P. K. et al. (2015). "Awe, the Small Self, and Prosocial Behavior." *Journal of Personality and Social Psychology.*
2. Yaden, D. B. et al. (2016). "The Overview Effect: Awe and Self-Transcendent Experience in Space Flight." *Psychology of Consciousness: Theory, Research, and Practice* 3(1), 1–11. Examined first-person accounts from astronauts describing the cognitive and emotional shift experienced upon seeing Earth from orbit. See also: White, F. (1987). *The Overview Effect: Space Exploration and Human Evolution.* Houghton Mifflin. The original account that named and documented the phenomenon through interviews with astronauts.
3. The "after-effect" of digital saturation toward tangible engagement is documented across multiple studies. See: Dittmar, H. et al. (2014). "Consumer Culture, Identity and Well-Being." *Psychology Press.* Also: Turkle, S. (2015). *Reclaiming Conversation.* Penguin. Both document renewed hunger for embodied experience following periods of digital immersion.
4. Etsy Seller Handbook. "What is Etsy's stance on AI creations?" Etsy's official policy addressing AI-generated products on its marketplace and its commitment to handmade, human-created goods.
5. Monroy, M. & Keltner, D. (2023). "Awe as a Pathway to Mental and Physical Health." *Perspectives on Psychological Science*, 18(2), 309–320. First published online in 2022. https://doi.org/10.1177/17456916221094856.

6. Motoori Norinaga developed mono no aware as the central concept of his *Genji* criticism in the eighteenth century. See Marra, M. F. (2007). *The Poetics of Motoori Norinaga.* University of Hawai'i Press.

11. The New Human Contract with AI

1. Eno, B. & Schmidt, P. (1975). *Oblique Strategies: Over One Hundred Worthwhile Dilemmas.* Self-published. The deck originally comprised 113 cards, each carrying an aphoristic instruction designed to interrupt habitual creative approaches. Multiple editions have been produced since, and digital versions are freely available. The project grew from parallel thinking between Eno and Schmidt about the role of constraints in creative work.
2. The recording of *"Heroes"* at Hansa Tonstudio, West Berlin, in 1977 is documented in Buckley, D. (1999). *Strange Fascination: David Bowie, The Definitive Story.* Virgin Books. Eno's use of the Oblique Strategies during the sessions, and his method of handing cards to musicians to disrupt their habitual approaches, is described in Tamm, E. (1995). *Brian Eno: His Music and the Vertical Color of Sound.* Da Capo Press.
3. Robert Fripp's guitar approach on the title track "Heroes" is documented in Tamm, E. (1995). *Brian Eno: His Music and the Vertical Color of Sound.* Da Capo Press. Fripp's three-distance feedback technique, combined with Eno's ring modulator processing, created the sustained guitar layers that define the track — a sound that emerged from deliberate constraint rather than conventional technique.
4. Eno, B. (1996). *A Year with Swollen Appendices.* Faber & Faber. Eno's diaries and essays document his long-running argument that sophisticated tools require deliberate friction to prevent them from homogenising creative output. See also: Kelly, K. (1995). "Gossip Is Philosophy." *Wired*, May 1995, for Eno's thinking on creativity and technology in interview form.
5. Sharma, M. et al. (2024). "Towards Understanding Sycophancy in Language Models." *Proceedings of ICLR 2024.* Found that AI assistants consistently adjust responses to match user views rather than prioritising accuracy. arXiv:2310.13548.
6. Mayer, R. C., Davis, J. H. & Schoorman, F. D. (1995). "An Integrative Model of Organizational Trust." *Academy of Management Review.* The foundational model establishing that perceived integrity, including willingness to disagree, is a key component of trust.
7. McGuire, J., De Cremer, D. & Van de Cruys, T. (2024). "Establishing the Importance of Co-creation and Self-efficacy in Creative Collaboration with Artificial Intelligence." *Scientific Reports* 14, 18525. Participants who co-created from their own material reported greater creative self-efficacy and ownership of the result than those placed in the role of editing AI-generated output. See also Chapter 7, note 9.
8. Bureau d'Enquêtes et d'Analyses pour la sécurité de l'aviation civile. (2012). *Final Report on the accident on 1st June 2009 to the Airbus A330-203, flight AF 447.* All flight details and findings cited follow the report.
9. Bainbridge, L. (1983). "Ironies of Automation." *Automatica*, 19(6), 775–779.
10. Morris, W. (1884). "Useful Work versus Useless Toil." Argues that meaningful work, craft with purpose, was being destroyed by industrialisation, and that the destruction was not merely economic but spiritual.

BIBLIOGRAPHY

Andrews, Geoff. *The Slow Food Story: Politics and Pleasure*. McGill-Queen's University Press, 2008.

Bainbridge, Lisanne. "Ironies of Automation." *Automatica* 19, no. 6 (1983): 775–779.

Barasch, Alixandra. *See* Bhattacharjee, Amit.

BBC News. "Right to Repair Movement Gains Power in US and Europe." 6 July 2021. https://www.bbc.com/news/technology-57744091.

Beaty, Roger E., Yoed N. Kenett, Alexander P. Christensen, Monica D. Rosenberg, Mathias Benedek, Qunlin Chen, Andreas Fink, Jiang Qiu, Thomas R. Kwapil, Michael J. Kane, and Paul J. Silvia. "Robust Prediction of Individual Creative Ability from Brain Functional Connectivity." *Proceedings of the National Academy of Sciences* 115, no. 5 (2018): 1087–1092.

Bhattacharjee, Amit, Alixandra Barasch, and Klaus Wertenbroch. "Too Good to Be True? Imperfection as a Costly Signal of Authenticity." SSRN Working Paper, 2022. https://papers.ssrn.com/sol3/papers.cfm?abstract_id=3233792.

Bowman, David M. J. S. "The Impact of Aboriginal Landscape Burning on the Australian Biota." *New Phytologist* 140, no. 3 (1998): 385–410. https://doi.org/10.1046/j.1469-8137.1998.00289.x.

Bredius, Abraham. "A New Vermeer." *The Burlington Magazine* 71, no. 416 (1937): 210–211.

Brown, Brené. *Daring Greatly: How the Courage to Be Vulnerable Transforms the Way We Live, Love, Parent, and Lead*. Gotham Books, 2012.

Brown, Brené. *The Gifts of Imperfection: Let Go of Who You Think You're Supposed to Be and Embrace Who You Are*. Hazelden, 2010.

Buckley, David. *Strange Fascination: David Bowie, The Definitive Story*. Virgin Books, 1999.

Bureau d'Enquêtes et d'Analyses. *Final Report on the Accident on 1st June 2009 to the Airbus A330-203, Flight AF 447*. BEA, 2012.

Cameron, Julia. *The Artist's Way: A Spiritual Path to Higher Creativity*. Tarcher/Perigee, 1992.

"Carlo Petrini Joins Anti-McDonald's Demonstration in Paris." Slow Food. https://www.slowfood.com/carlo-petrini-joins-anti-mcdonalds-demonstration-in-paris/.

Carr, Ian. *Keith Jarrett: The Man and His Music*. Da Capo Press, 1992.

Carter, K. Codell. *Childbed Fever: A Scientific Biography of Ignaz Semmelweis*. Transaction Publishers, 1994.

Catmull, Ed, and Amy Wallace. *Creativity, Inc.: Overcoming the Unseen Forces That Stand in the Way of True Inspiration*. Random House, 2014.

Chamberlain, Elizabeth. "Right to Repair Laws Have Now Been Introduced in All 50 US States." iFixit, 24 February 2025. https://www.ifixit.com/News/108371/right-to-repair-laws-have-now-been-introduced-in-all-50-us-states.

Chamberlain, Rebecca, Caitlin Mullin, Bram Scheerlinck, and Johan Wagemans. "Putting the Art in Artificial: Aesthetic Responses to Computer-Generated Art." *Psychology of Aesthetics, Creativity, and the Arts* 12, no. 2 (2018): 177–192.

Chinen, Nate. *Playing Changes: Jazz for the New Century*. Pantheon Books, 2018.

Ciechanowski, Leon, Aleksandra Przegalinska, Mikolaj Magnuski, and Peter Gloor. "In the Shades of the Uncanny Valley: An Experimental Study of Human-Chatbot Interaction." *Future Generation Computer Systems* 92 (2019): 539–548. https://doi.org/10.1016/j.future.2018.01.055.

Csikszentmihalyi, Mihaly. *Flow: The Psychology of Optimal Experience*. Harper & Row, 1990.

Csikszentmihalyi, Mihaly, and Reed Larson. "Validity and Reliability of the Experience-Sampling Method." *Journal of Nervous and Mental Disease* 175, no. 9 (1987): 526–536. https://doi.org/10.1097/00005053-198709000-00004.

Dal Co, Francesco. *Tadao Ando: Complete Works*. Phaidon, 1995.

Dickman, Chris, et al. *After the Catastrophe: A Blueprint for a Conservation Response to Large-Scale Ecological Disaster*. University of Sydney, 2020.

Dittmar, Helga, et al. *Consumer Culture, Identity and Well-Being*. Psychology Press, 2014.

Dolnick, Edward. *The Forger's Spell: A True Story of Vermeer, Nazis, and the Greatest Art Hoax of the Twentieth Century*. HarperCollins, 2008.

Doshi, Anil R., and Oliver P. Hauser. "Generative AI Enhances Individual Creativity but Reduces the Collective Diversity of Novel Content." *Science Advances* 10, no. 28 (2024): eadn5290. https://doi.org/10.1126/sciadv.adn5290.

ECM Records. *The Köln Concert*. ECM 1064/65. Recorded 24 January 1975. Released 1975.

Eno, Brian. *A Year with Swollen Appendices*. Faber & Faber, 1996.

Eno, Brian, and Peter Schmidt. *Oblique Strategies: Over One Hundred Worthwhile Dilemmas*. Self-published, 1975.

Ericsson, K. Anders, Ralf T. Krampe, and Clemens Tesch-Römer. "The Role of Deliberate Practice in the Acquisition of Expert Performance." *Psychological Review* 100, no. 3 (1993): 363–406.

Ericsson, K. Anders, and Robert Pool. *Peak: Secrets from the New Science of Expertise*. Houghton Mifflin Harcourt, 2016.

Etsy. "What Is Etsy's Stance on AI Creations?" Etsy Seller Handbook.

Flematti, Gavin R., Emilio L. Ghisalberti, Kingsley W. Dixon, and Robert D. Trengove. "A Compound from Smoke That Promotes Seed Germination." *Science* 305, no. 5686 (2004): 977. https://doi.org/10.1126/science.1099944.

Gelb, David, dir. *Jiro Dreams of Sushi*. Magnolia Pictures, 2011.

Grove, David, and Basil I. Panzer. *Resolving Traumatic Memories: Metaphors and Symbols in Psychotherapy*. Irvington Publishers, 1989.

Hall, Johnathon, and Damian Schofield. "The Value of Creativity: Human Produced Art vs. AI-Generated Art." *Art and Design Review* 13, no. 1 (2025): 65–88. https://doi.org/10.4236/adr.2025.131005.

Hayes, Bill. *Insomniac City: New York, Oliver Sacks, and Me*. Bloomsbury, 2017.

Herndon, Holly. *PROTO*. 4AD Records, 2019.

Holster, Jacob. "Augmenting Music Education Through AI: Practical Applications of

ChatGPT." *Music Educators Journal* 110, no. 4 (2024): 36–42. *https://doi.org/10.1177/00274321241255938*.

Horton, C. Blaine, Jr., Michael W. White, and Sheena S. Iyengar. "Bias Against AI Art Can Enhance Perceptions of Human Creativity." *Scientific Reports* 13 (2023). https://doi.org/10.1038/s41598-023-45202-3.

Immordino-Yang, Mary Helen, Joanna A. Christodoulou, and Vanessa Singh. "Rest Is Not Idleness: Implications of the Brain's Default Mode for Human Development and Education." *Perspectives on Psychological Science* 7, no. 4 (2012): 352–364.

Inzlicht, Michael, Amitai Shenhav, and Christopher Y. Olivola. "The Effort Paradox: Effort Is Both Costly and Valued." *Trends in Cognitive Sciences* 22, no. 4 (2018): 337–349. https://doi.org/10.1016/j.tics.2018.01.007.

Jafari, Shakila. "Machine Learning in Human Creativity." Master's dissertation, NOVA Information Management School, Universidade NOVA de Lisboa, 2023.

Jones, Rhys. "Fire-Stick Farming." *Australian Natural History* 16, no. 7 (1969): 224–228.

Kelly, Kevin. "Gossip Is Philosophy." *Wired*, May 1995.

Keltner, Dacher. *Awe: The New Science of Everyday Wonder and Why It Has the Power to Heal, Connect, and Inspire*. Penguin, 2023.

Kemske, Bonnie. *Kintsugi: The Poetic Mend*. Herbert Press, 2017.

Kilbracken, John. *Van Meegeren: Master Forger*. Scribner's, 1967.

Kimmerer, Robin Wall. *Braiding Sweetgrass: Indigenous Wisdom, Scientific Knowledge, and the Teachings of Plants*. Milkweed Editions, 2013.

Kleon, Austin. *Keep Going: 10 Ways to Stay Creative in Good Times and Bad*. Workman Publishing, 2019.

Kleon, Austin. *Show Your Work! 10 Ways to Share Your Creativity and Get Discovered*. Workman Publishing, 2014.

Kleon, Austin. *Steal Like an Artist: 10 Things Nobody Told You About Being Creative*. Workman Publishing, 2012.

Köbis, Nils, and Luca D. Mossink. "Artificial Intelligence versus Maya Angelou: Experimental Evidence That People Cannot Differentiate AI-Generated from Human-Written Poetry." *Computers in Human Behavior* 114 (2021): 106553.

Koren, Leonard. *Wabi-Sabi for Artists, Designers, Poets and Philosophers*. Stone Bridge Press, 1994.

Kramer, Matt. *Making Sense of Burgundy*. William Morrow, 1990.

Kumar, Harsh, Jonathan Vincentius, Ewan Jordan, and Ashton Anderson. "Human Creativity in the Age of LLMs: Randomized Experiments on Divergent and Convergent Thinking." *Proceedings of CHI* 2025. ACM, 2025.

Lakoff, George, and Mark Johnson. *Philosophy in the Flesh: The Embodied Mind and Its Challenge to Western Thought*. Basic Books, 1999.

Lee, John D., and Katrina A. See. "Trust in Automation: Designing for Appropriate Reliance." *Human Factors* 46, no. 1 (2004): 50–80.

Loftus, Elizabeth F. "Planting Misinformation in the Human Mind: A 30-Year Investigation of the Malleability of Memory." *Learning & Memory* 12, no. 4 (2005): 361–366. https://doi.org/10.1101/lm.94705.

Loftus, Elizabeth F., and John C. Palmer. "Reconstruction of Automobile Destruction:

An Example of the Interaction Between Language and Memory." *Journal of Verbal Learning and Verbal Behavior* 13, no. 5 (1974): 585–589.

Loftus, Elizabeth F., and Jacqueline E. Pickrell. "The Formation of False Memories." *Psychiatric Annals* 25, no. 12 (1995): 720–725.

Lowry, Christopher A., et al. "Identification of an Immune-Responsive Mesolimbocortical Serotonergic System: Potential Role in Regulation of Emotional Behavior." *Neuroscience* 146, no. 2 (2007): 756–772.

MacCarthy, Fiona. *William Morris: A Life for Our Time*. Faber & Faber, 1994.

Marra, Michael F. *The Poetics of Motoori Norinaga: A Hermeneutical Journey*. University of Hawai'i Press, 2007.

Marsen, Sky. "The Role of Meaning in Human Thinking." *Journal of Evolution and Technology* 17, no. 1 (2008): 45–58.

Mayer, Roger C., James H. Davis, and F. David Schoorman. "An Integrative Model of Organizational Trust." *Academy of Management Review* 20, no. 3 (1995): 709–734.

McCurry, Justin. "'World's Best Sushi Restaurant' Stripped of Its Three Michelin Stars." *The Guardian*, 26 November 2019.

McGuire, Jack, David De Cremer, and Tim Van de Cruys. "Establishing the Importance of Co-creation and Self-efficacy in Creative Collaboration with Artificial Intelligence." *Scientific Reports* 14 (2024): 18525.

Menon, Vinod. "20 Years of the Default Mode Network: A Review and Synthesis." *Neuron* 111, no. 16 (2023): 2469–2487. https://doi.org/10.1016/j.neuron.2023.04.023.

Metz, Cade. "In Two Moves, AlphaGo and Lee Sedol Redefined the Future." *Wired*, 16 March 2016.

Microsoft AI Economy Institute. *Global AI Adoption in 2025*. Microsoft, January 2026.

Monroy, Maria, and Dacher Keltner. "Awe as a Pathway to Mental and Physical Health." *Perspectives on Psychological Science* 18, no. 2 (2023): 309–320.

Mori, Masahiro. "Bukimi no Tani" [The Uncanny Valley]. Energy 7, no. 4 (1970): 33–35. English translation: Mori, Masahiro, Karl F. MacDorman, and Norri Kageki. "The Uncanny Valley [From the Field]." *IEEE Robotics & Automation Magazine* 19, no. 2 (2012): 98–100. https://doi.org/10.1109/MRA.2012.2192811.

Morris, William. "The Beauty of Life." Lecture delivered to the Birmingham Society of Arts and School of Design, 1880.

Morris, William. *News from Nowhere and Other Writings*. Penguin Classics, 1993.

Morris, William. "Useful Work versus Useless Toil." *Lecture delivered to the Hampstead Liberal Club*, 1884.

Murphy, Gillian, et al. "Lost in the Mall Again: A Preregistered Replication and Extension of Loftus & Pickrell (1995)." *Memory* 31, no. 6 (2023). https://doi.org/10.1080/09658211.2023.2198327.

Newport, Cal. *Deep Work: Rules for Focused Success in a Distracted World*. Grand Central Publishing, 2016.

Nguyen, C. Thi. "Autonomy and Aesthetic Engagement." *Mind* 129, no. 516 (2020): 1127–1156.

Nilsson, Lisa. "Mio Heki: Kintsugi Artist and Urushi Master." *Kyoto Journal*, August

2018. https://kyotojournal.org/creative-kyoto/mio-heki-kintsugi-artist-and-urushi-master/.

Norton, Michael I., Daniel Mochon, and Dan Ariely. "The IKEA Effect: When Labor Leads to Love." *Journal of Consumer Psychology* 22, no. 3 (2012): 453–460. https://doi.org/10.1016/j.jcps.2011.08.002.

Nuland, Sherwin B. *The Doctors' Plague: Germs, Childbed Fever, and the Strange Story of Ignaz Semmelweis*. W. W. Norton & Company, 2003.

Ophir, Eyal, Clifford Nass, and Anthony D. Wagner. "Cognitive Control in Media Multitaskers." *Proceedings of the National Academy of Sciences* 106, no. 37 (2009): 15583–15587.

Oppezzo, Marily, and Daniel L. Schwartz. "Give Your Ideas Some Legs: The Positive Effect of Walking on Creative Thinking." *Journal of Experimental Psychology: Learning*, Memory, and Cognition 40, no. 4 (2014): 1142–1152.

Peng, Sida, Eirini Kalliamvakou, Peter Cihon, and Mert Demirer. "The Impact of AI on Developer Productivity: Evidence from GitHub Copilot." arXiv preprint arXiv:2302.06590, 2023.

Piff, Paul K., Pia Dietze, Matthew Feinberg, Daniel M. Stancato, and Dacher Keltner. "Awe, the Small Self, and Prosocial Behavior." *Journal of Personality and Social Psychology* 108, no. 6 (2015): 883–899.

Pitelka, Morgan. *Handmade Culture: Raku Potters, Patrons, and Tea Practitioners in Japan*. University of Hawai'i Press, 2005.

Plato. *Meno. Translated by W. K. C. Guthrie. In Collected Dialogues of Plato, edited by Edith Hamilton and Huntington Cairns*. Princeton University Press, 1961.

Ragot, Martin, Nicolas Martin, and Salomé Cojean. "AI-Generated vs. Human Artworks: A Perception Bias Towards Artificial Intelligence?" *Extended Abstracts of the* 2020 CHI Conference on Human Factors in Computing Systems. ACM, 2020. https://doi.org/10.1145/3334480.3382892.

Recording Industry Association of America. *2022 Year-End Music Industry Revenue Report*. RIAA, 2023. riaa.com.

Recording Industry Association of America. *2023 Year-End Music Industry Revenue Report*. RIAA, 2024. riaa.com.

Rilke, Rainer Maria. *Letters to a Young Poet*. Translated by M. D. Herter Norton. W. W. Norton, 1934.

Roland Berger. "iFixit Is Fighting for Consumers' Right to Repair." 23 October 2022. https://www.rolandberger.com/en/Insights/Publications/iFixit-is-fighting-for-consumers-right-to-repair.html.

Sacks, Oliver. *On the Move: A Life*. Alfred A. Knopf, 2015.

Semmelweis, Ignaz Philipp. *Die Ätiologie, der Begriff und die Prophylaxis des Kindbettfiebers* [The Etiology, Concept and Prophylaxis of Childbed Fever]. Hartleben, 1861.

Shapiro, Lawrence. *Embodied Cognition*. Routledge, 2011.

Sharma, Mrinank, et al. "Towards Understanding Sycophancy in Language Models." *Proceedings of ICLR* 2024. arXiv:2310.13548.

"S. Korean Workers Are Embracing AI Faster than Internet, or Any Tech Before." *The Korea Herald*, 2026.

"The Slow Food Movement and McDonald's: A Surprising Link." *Time*, 15 December 2014. https://time.com/3626290/mcdonalds-slow-food/.

Sparrow, Betsy, Jenny Liu, and Daniel M. Wegner. "Google Effects on Memory: Cognitive Consequences of Having Information at Our Fingertips." *Science* 333, no. 6043 (2011): 776–778.

Steffensen, Victor. *Fire Country: How Indigenous Fire Management Could Help Save Australia*. Hardie Grant Travel, 2020.

Stellar, Jennifer E., et al. "Self-Transcendent Emotions and Their Social Functions: Compassion, Gratitude, and Awe Bind Us to Others Through Prosociality." *Emotion Review* 9, no. 3 (2017): 200–207.

Tamm, Eric. *Brian Eno: His Music and the Vertical Color of Sound*. Da Capo Press, 1995.

Tompkins, Penny, and James Lawley. *Metaphors in Mind: Transformation Through Symbolic Modelling*. The Developing Company Press, 2000.

Turkle, Sherry. *Reclaiming Conversation: The Power of Talk in a Digital Age*. Penguin, 2015.

Vallor, Shannon. *The AI Mirror: How to Reclaim Our Humanity in an Age of Machine Thinking*. Oxford University Press, 2024.

van der Meer, Audrey L. H., and F. R. van der Weel. "Only Three Fingers Write, but the Whole Brain Works: A High-Density EEG Study Showing Advantages of Drawing Over Typing for Learning." *Frontiers in Psychology* 8 (2017): 706. https://doi.org/10.3389/fpsyg.2017.00706.

Ward, Michael, et al. "Impact of 2019–2020 Mega-fires on Australian Fauna Habitat." *Nature Ecology & Evolution* 4 (2020): 1321–1326.

Wegner, Daniel M. "Transactive Memory: A Contemporary Analysis of the Group Mind." In *Theories of Group Behavior*, edited by Brian Mullen and George R. Goethals, 185–208. Springer, 1987.

Weizenbaum, Joseph. *Computer Power and Human Reason: From Judgment to Calculation*. W. H. Freeman, 1976.

Weizenbaum, Joseph. "ELIZA: A Computer Program for the Study of Natural Language Communication Between Man and Machine." *Communications of the ACM* 9, no. 1 (1966): 36–45. https://doi.org/10.1145/365153.365168.

White, Frank. *The Overview Effect: Space Exploration and Human Evolution*. Houghton Mifflin, 1987.

Williams, Margery. *The Velveteen Rabbit, or How Toys Become Real*. Illustrated by William Nicholson. George H. Doran Company, 1922.

Yaden, David B., et al. "The Overview Effect: Awe and Self-Transcendent Experience in Space Flight." *Psychology of Consciousness: Theory*, Research, and Practice 3, no. 1 (2016): 1–11. https://doi.org/10.1037/cns0000086.

Yee, Nick, and Jeremy Bailenson. "The Proteus Effect: The Effect of Transformed Self-Representation on Behavior." *Human Communication Research* 33, no. 3 (2007): 271–290.

Yee, Nick, Jeremy N. Bailenson, and Nicolas Ducheneaut. "The Proteus Effect: Implications of Transformed Digital Self-Representation on Online and Offline Behavior." *Communication Research* 36, no. 2 (2009): 285–312.

Yonhap News Agency. Lee Sedol retirement interview, 27 November 2019.

Zhang, Yunhao, and Renée Richardson Gosline. "Human Favoritism, Not AI Aversion: People's Perceptions (and Bias) Toward Generative AI, Human Experts, and Human–GAI Collaboration in Persuasive Content Generation." *Judgment and Decision Making* 18 (2023): e41. https://doi.org/10.1017/jdm.2023.37.

Zhou, Yizhen, and Hideaki Kawabata. "Eyes Can Tell: Assessment of Implicit Attitudes Toward AI Art." *i-Perception* 14 (2023): 20416695231209846. https://doi.org/10.1177/20416695231209846.

INDEX

N

O

P

Q

R

S

ABOUT THE AUTHOR

Anna McPhee has been building for the web since before Google existed. She's watched every wave of technology arrive, get over-hyped, partially deliver, and reshape the world anyway.

With over twenty years as a full-stack developer, she spent a decade working nomadically before finally admitting that having a fixed address is occasionally useful. She now speaks at conferences on emerging agentic technologies and blogs prolifically about AI.

What Machines Can't Replace is her attempt to say the quiet part loud before everyone else catches up. You can keep up with Anna's work at https://anna.kiwi

A SMALL REQUEST

I published this book through E. E. Press, my own imprint, whose entire staff is me. So there is no marketing department and no advertising budget to speak of, and if the book reaches new readers, that will mostly be because people like yourself, who liked it, went on and said so somewhere.

If the book gave you something, a review wherever you bought it would help me more than anything. After a whole book about the worth of words a real person chose to write, you can imagine how much more a human review means to me than any advertising could.

And if you would like to tell me what the book stirred up in you, please write to me at hello@anna.kiwi. The Conversation Starters at the end of each chapter were always an invitation, and the invitation stands.

Please also come and join me in my newsletter by opting in at whatmachinescantreplace.com/hello

Thank you for reading.

www.ingramcontent.com/pod-product-compliance
Lightning Source LLC
LaVergne TN
LVHW100302210926
848480LV00003B/1001
9781764584814